yes—but also filled with humour, love, and bursting with life. Reid's story, gorgeously told by Bascaramurty, will make you rethink what it means to be a spouse, a parent, and a friend." **Ann Hui, author of** *Chop Suey Nation*

"*This Is Not the End of Me* is a beautifully rendered story of vulnerability and compassion. Dakshana Bascaramurty delicately sheds light on the complexities of mortality, while showing the value and importance of accepting our own fragility." **Iain Reid, author of** *Foe*

"Equal parts beautiful, heartbreaking, and inspiring, this is a book you'll be thinking about long after you finish reading." **Robyn Doolittle, author of** *Had It Coming*

"An exquisite, heartbreaking exploration of life and death. Dakshana Bascaramurty expertly delves inside one family's multifaceted being, its wrestle with fate and love and degeneration, bringing the reader along with her. I dare you to read this and not be overcome by the need to gnaw at life, the desire to design your final hours, your commemoration. A true celebration of an unremitting spirit." **Anna Mehler Paperny, author of** *Hello I Want to Die Please Fix Me*

"*This Is Not the End of Me* is a book for anyone who loves fiercely, with dedication and passion and loyalty to the end. How do our stories end? What matters most is who we are with while our stories are being written. Dakshana Bascaramurty lays out, in astonishing detail, the lengths we go to for the people we love. This book is about the constant caring, raging and measuring that go into a family's balancing act, a bid to help Layton Reid stay alive longer with his loving family, tensions and all. Layton's constant documentation and attempt to pass stories forward becomes a collaboration of sorts with the author, who lays out his tenacity in a clear-eyed story. This is Layton's legacy and it's a tribute to caregivers, survivors, parents and people who love. What the author has done with his story is a tribute, not just to Layton and his whole family, but to life and love itself." **Hannah Sung, journalist**

"*This Is Not the End of Me* is a hard read. You think you know how it ends. You do. But, also, you do not. Finding meaning, love, hope and resilience at life's end is a cruel twist of fate. It is also, ironically, life saving. This heart-wrenching journey lays bare the fact that our lives, whenever they may come to an end, are never complete. I, for one, find a certain comfort in that." **Mark Sakamoto, author of *Forgiveness***

"*This Is Not the End of Me* is a deeply human story about cancer, an unorthodox treatment, and a man on his last walk. But it's so much more than that—a beautifully real and inspiring journey filled with courage and love." **Charlotte Gill, author of *Eating Dirt***

Praise for

this is not the end of me

"*This Is Not the End of Me* is a profoundly moving book about living wrapped in a book about dying. An immersive, beautifully detailed portrait of a young family learning to cope with illness, it will resonate long after the final page is read." **Elizabeth Renzetti, author of *Shrewed***

"How do you continue living even as you prepare for death? In the case of Layton Reid, who died at 37, a terminal cancer diagnosis led him to try to condense decades of love, marriage and fatherhood into a mere handful of years. Intimate and unvarnished, Dakshana Bascaramurty's *This Is Not the End of Me* faithfully chronicles her friend's reckoning with his mortality and legacy. Bearing witness to the journey of Layton, his wife Candace, and the couple's families, Bascaramurty tenderly captures moments of compassion and grace, as well as denial, anger and sorrow. This is a book about the profound, fragile and beautiful condition of being human." **Rachel Giese, author of *Boys: What It Means to Become a Man*, winner of the Writers' Trust of Canada Shaughnessy Cohen Prize for Political Writing**

"Cancer patients are often portrayed as heroes and survivors, as caricatures. Dakshana Bascaramurty provides an intimate glimpse of the more common, not-always-rosy reality: The loneliness, fear, desperation, grieving and loss experienced by cancer patients and their families. *This Is Not the End of Me* is not always an easy read but a necessary one—an enlightening exploration of coming to terms with mortality." **André Picard, health columnist, *The Globe and Mail*, author of *Matters of Life and Death***

"Who would have predicted that a life apparently doomed by cancer held so much future richness? Somehow, Dakshana Bascaramurty did. Her panoptic reporting, her steady attention to every detail in multiple lives, her calm, clear sentences, and most of all her astonishing patience over the years it took for Layton Reid's story to unfold, have created a book no one will forget." **Ian Brown, author of *Sixty***

"Dakshana Bascaramurty has written a book as captivating in its frankness as the delightfully no-BS man at its core. It touches your heart. It makes you grapple with essential questions about how we die and live. And, like Layton Reid, it's much funnier than you'd expect under the circumstances." **Daniel Dale, CNN**

"With tremendous compassion and insight, Dakshana Bascaramurty tells the story of Layton Reid and his extraordinary approach to life after a terminal cancer diagnosis. This is an honest, intimate story about death and dying that is devastating,

Dakshana Bascaramurty

this is not the end of me

LESSONS ON LIVING FROM A DYING MAN

McClelland & Stewart

Library and Archives Canada Cataloguing in Publication

Title: This is not the end of me : lessons on living from a dying man /
Dakshana Bascaramurty.
Names: Bascaramurty, Dakshana, author.
Identifiers: Canadiana (print) 20190162171 | Canadiana (ebook) 20190162228 |
ISBN 9780771009631 (softcover) | ISBN 9780771009648 (EPUB)
Subjects: LCSH: Reid, Layton, 1979-2017. | LCSH: Reid, Layton, 1979-2017—Family. |
LCSH: Reid, Layton, 1979-2017—Health. | LCSH: Cancer—Patients—Canada—
Biography. | LCSH: Cancer—Patients—Family relationships—Canada.
Classification: LCC RC265.6.R45 B37 2020 | DDC 362.19699/40092—dc23

The lyrics on page 230 from "Barcelona" and "No One's Gonna Love You (Quite Like I
Do)" from the album *Compostela* by Jenn Grant; on page 244 from "Barcelona" from the
album *Compostela* by Jenn Grant; and on page 258 from "Dog Fight" from the album
Paradise by Jenn Grant are reprinted by permission.

Cover design by Rachel Cooper
Text design by Leah Springate
Cover art: (background) Hamed Daram/Unsplash; (sweatshirt) airdone/Shutterstock
Images; (flowers) Tetra images/Getty Images
Typeset in Bembo by M&S, Toronto
Printed and bound in Canada

McClelland & Stewart,
a division of Penguin Random House Canada Limited,
a Penguin Random House Company
www.penguinrandomhouse.ca

2   3   4   5   24   23   22   21   20

Penguin
Random House
McCLELLAND & STEWART

For Appa, who I wish could've read this

this is not the end of me

one

Layton Reid was curled up like the letter S on the floor of the hospital bathroom. He tried not to come in contact with the toilet, but the lack of floor space meant his head—covered by the hood on his grey sweatshirt—was touching the white porcelain bowl. A cloth grocery bag served as a makeshift pillow. He was spent, largely because of this new, extreme medical therapy he was trying—one that included five self-administered coffee enemas per day. But also because he and his wife, Candace, were now entering their seventeenth hour since her first contraction began, kicking off their long and mutually painful wait for their son to be born.

As Layton clenched the muscles around his butt, trying his best to hold in the 225 millilitres of coffee he had just inserted via a long tube connected to a bucket, Candace was in the next room summoning her own muscles to work in the opposite direction and push a human out through her vaginal canal. It was the first time in a long while that she was in worse physical pain than her husband. When the really bad contractions seized her, she'd pick up the sonogram of her son that was on the table beside her bed and focus her attention on it. *Remember*, she told herself, *at the end of this tunnel of agony will be a baby. Your baby.*

Like most first-time parents, Candace and Layton went to the hospital soon after Candace's contractions began and were told by a no-nonsense triage nurse to come back when the spasms were much closer together. They spent a few hours at the coffee shop downstairs, both of them writhing in pain— Candace, from labour; Layton, from digestive issues. Enema time came around and Candace still hadn't been admitted, so Layton wandered into a tiny public bathroom the size of a utility closet to do the deed. In that tight space, the bucket fell off the sink and hot liquid poured down his back. He could hear Candace outside, pacing the hallway, gritting her teeth through contractions, letting passersby know the bathroom Layton was in was occupied.

Finally, Candace was admitted, but the hours ticked on and she was told it still wasn't time to start pushing. She was ready to jump off a balcony. To help ease the pain and move things along, nurses put her in a bath. Candace told Layton to sleep in her hospital room bed. A few feet apart, both were in their own private agony.

For his next enema, Layton was in a slightly more comfortable bathroom—at least he had a thin white towel wedged between himself and the cold floor. Instead of standing over

Candace's bed to document her delivery with his iPad's camera, he'd turned it on himself, recording a video letter to his son, who was still stuck somewhere in his wife's birth canal.

"I feel terrible because I have to sit here and do this while she's out there but, um, it is what it is, man. She wanted me to be here, so . . . ," he said to the camera, his voice gravelly and his eyes squinting from the lack of sleep, the anxiety. Candace moaned deeply, so loud and low it reverberated through the door. Layton, who was lying on his right side, turned his head towards where the noise came from, straining to hear a conversation between Candace and a nurse.

"They're asking where I am," he said, laughing. "What are you going to do?"

He explained to his baby that Candace had been in severe pain for some time now, and that his mother-in-law had done much of the work supporting Candace through labour since he himself was not physically up to the task.

"My wife is out there in pain and I need to be out there, man," he said, breathing deeply.

"But I will be soon. And we're going to meet you soon, my man."

He wasn't supposed to have a child. Or a wife. Or a mortgage. Or a permanent address, even. Nor was he supposed to be fighting for his own life at the exact moment his son was starting his. But here they all were.

Layton was six foot two and lanky. He wore jeans that were slightly too big and baggy hoodies to add bulk to his frame. His eyes were blue and warm and his hair was the colour of a russet potato. When he smiled, he looked bashful, like a ten-year-old with a crush. He cursed a lot, but there was never any malice in anything he said. He liked to put things up his nose: scrunched-up tissues, pencils, his fingers. He was thirty-three. He did not seem thirty-three.

The decade that preceded that moment of him squirming on the floor and Candace squirming in the bed next door had been a whirlwind. Layton was never in one place or state of mind. He was always dreaming, planning, and leaving—he and Candace had dated on and off while he travelled the world, working odd jobs: he went from England to Australia to South Korea to South Africa to Brazil and finally back to Canada. *Marriage* was never a word that crossed his lips, let alone *kids*, and Halifax was always going to be the hometown of his past, not his present or his future.

But then, a melanoma diagnosis anchored him: to Candace, and to Halifax. He got married, went into remission, and Candace got pregnant. But then the routine scans Layton did every six months showed tumours in his lung and stomach. The cancer had come back: Stage IV this time, the last, worst stage of the disease.

An appointment to meet with Layton's oncologist, Mary Davis, was hastily scheduled. Dr. Davis—or Mimi, as patients liked to call her—was a tiny woman, whose frame was swallowed up by the standard-issue lab coats she wore. She had a soothing way of speaking, like a kindergarten teacher at nap time.

In that first meeting after the scans, Layton couldn't really grasp what she was saying. He could tell from her body language that this was serious. She explained all the treatment options, something about surgery, more scans she wanted to order. But her soft words blurred together. Layton felt like he had left his body and was standing somewhere else in the room, watching this scene unfold. He grew numb as Mimi continued on about this type of surgery and that type of test and exposure to radiation. He asked her, point blank, where he stood.

"Sweetie, would you like to talk about living and dying?" she asked gently. There was an unusual brokenness in Mimi's tone. Her question was void of optimism.

No, he would not like to talk about living and dying.

She tried to offer him hope: a man from Prince Edward Island was diagnosed with Stage IV melanoma and was still alive, years later, she said. But Layton had heard of this "miracle" case already—the possibility of living years after a Stage IV diagnosis is so rare that they trotted this guy out as an example every time. His heart sank. He slumped forward and cried. Mimi knew that a patient like Layton could expect to live for about ten months. But he stopped her before she got a chance to tell him that. He made it clear he wasn't interested in statistics.

She stood a few inches away to examine his lymph nodes as Layton thought about the tiny heart beating deep within Candace's belly. That strange, beautiful blob he'd recently seen on a sonogram. He asked her if he would meet his son.

"When is your wife due?" Mimi asked.

"In three months," he replied.

She paused. "I think it's very likely you will meet your son."

When Layton went home, he wrote that down: it felt like a goal now. Even if everything went to hell after that, he was going to make it through the next three months. The next morning, he opened up the document that he had been logging letters to his son in and began typing.

alright little man. got some shitty news last night. i didn't mention it before because we're really just trying to forget about it but i was pretty sick a few years ago. i had some surgeries and went on this nasty medication that made me feel like crap for a while but all seemed to be going good until the results of my yearly scan came up with some spots on my liver and lungs yesterday. to be honest it kind of rocked our world. we're not sure the ins and outs of it yet until we meet with our oncologist mimi davis tomorrow but it looks like we're in for a fight. radiation, maybe chemo, hopefully surgery. we all just want to get these little spots out of my body so that i'm super fit and healthy enough to take care of you, my man. you're due in like three months which is crazy to think. your mom has a big belly now and she feels you move around a lot. she looks beautiful. we can't wait to meet you. still haven't figured out a name for you but that will come soon, we'll probably have to meet you first to see what you look like. it's a bummer you can't pick your own name. mine is layton by the way. i was named after my grandfather (your great-grandfather). i used to not dig it so much but these days i'm glad it's different than other folks out there. to be honest we're all pretty scared right now. the uncertainty of having to deal with cancer (something that they'll hopefully have a cure for in your lifetime. hey, maybe mine!) is pretty heavy. there's a good possibility that i'll have to cancel many of my weddings (i'm a wedding photographer) this year and just focus on trying to get better. we might even have to sell/rent the house out to make up for me not working. it breaks my heart because this house is amazing and i just know you're going to love it. there are trails nearby and water and lots of places to explore. you'll see soon enough. today your mom and i have basically just been walking around in a haze feeling like this is all a dream but we make a good team. your mom is amazing. she's really good at keeping spirits high. when i'm upset she consoles me and when she's upset i console her. she is quite literally the love of my life. next to you of course. talk soon little man. we love you so much.

two

Before I had even spoken to him, I learned to see the world the way Layton did. I had fallen in love with his work while perusing his website from my home in Toronto as I planned my Halifax wedding in the fall of 2011. He wasn't one of those photographers who liked to edit out the unflattering, the sloppy, or the unexpected to create some pristine and unrealistic fairy-tale record of the day. I was charmed by his cheekiness, the way he captured those moments that happened on the fringes: the grandpa wiping out on the dance floor; the discarded package from a bride's wedding day Spanx; his own pants, split down the back while shooting a portrait session. He liked being around people on this occasion when they had permission to be genuine and passionate and emotional. Layton was a romantic but also an introvert, and he found himself living vicariously through his clients.

There was an unusual intimacy he and I built in a day. I didn't have a maid of honour, or even bridesmaids, so it was Layton who kept me company as I sat hidden away in a sari and too-tight braid ahead of the morning ceremony, who told me if I'd applied my eyeliner okay while I got ready for the reception, who shared an amused grin with me from across the room as we watched my dad fasten up his footwear of choice for his daughter's wedding day: a pair of white Velcro shoes. We traded cynicism and mortifying confessions and laughed till we were doubled over in his puppy hair–covered car, wheezing. It felt like the most tragic platonic missed connection when I had to fly back to Toronto after the wedding. Our relationship was officially over after he fulfilled his contractual obligation and mailed my husband and me a DVD of our photos.

But a year later, Layton's name unexpectedly popped up in my inbox. He told me about the melanoma diagnosis and revealed he was treating it with an extreme alternative therapy built around juicing and a strict vegan diet. I felt a wave of panic followed by helplessness. We weren't friends; we didn't live in the same city. I couldn't stop by his place for a friendly visit. I couldn't even drop off a bunch of kale on his doorstep. All I had were words. The way I responded to him must have been refreshing in some way because it triggered a chain of emails, and then regular video chats. At first, knowing I was a newspaper reporter, he sought advice on how he might document what he was going through for posterity, maybe in the form of a journal or an essay, something his son could read one day. Facing mortality was making him think about his own legacy. Our conversations became longer in the weeks that followed, covering more ground than the specifics of his day-to-day. He was pleased to find in me someone who asked real, sometimes uncomfortable questions and then simply listened, welcoming silences instead of rushing to fill them with trite platitudes.

In time, I realized he had a story worth sharing with a wider audience, and I wanted to be the one to tell it. I wanted to watch someone going through that evolution of coming to terms with their mortality from the front row, through each and every stumble.

The situation Layton was in had made him raw and open in a way I'd never seen in anyone else. And as I tried to figure out the nature of our relationship, I found that approaching our conversations as a journalist had the unexpected result of fast-tracking our friendship. Rather than slowly inching through the getting-to-know-you stage as most new acquaintances do, we launched right into the heavy, the deep, the uncomfortable. In just a few months, it felt like we'd laid the foundation for a decade's worth of friendship. My interest in him and his trust in me were rooted in the same place: we both documented the world in an unvarnished way, whether it was in pictures or in words. We hated sentimentality. And if things went "tits up," as Layton liked to say, it was important to both of us that the portrait of his life be uncompromising. He made it clear he wanted me to include all the ugly, embarrassing, and unflattering bits.

As our conversations became more frequent, it seemed like the next step in understanding and telling Layton's story—though I still wasn't sure what it was, exactly—was to fly out to

Halifax that winter to spend a few days at his house. I wanted to see, up close, what life looked like when it was being fought for so intensely.

I was admittedly nervous about meeting Candace for the first time. Would she be annoyed by my intrusion into her family's life? Would she be suspicious of my intentions, wondering why some woman she didn't know was suddenly so interested in her husband? But, as Layton had assured me on the phone, I had no reason to worry. Candace radiated warmth in a way that was so instant and so genuine it caught me off guard. She came down the stairs of their home in Halifax with a basket of laundry at her hip, her hair in rollers, and stopped mid-stride when she saw me and beamed with recognition, as though we were old friends from high school. She was one of those effortlessly pretty girl-next-door types who looks most beautiful after a ten-kilometre run, and Layton always spoke of her with this sense of awe, seemingly perplexed that she'd chosen him. While he travelled the world in his twenties, he broke up with her multiple times, but they always decided to get back together. He spent the first six years of his adult life as a night hotel manager in Cape Town, South Africa, an English teacher in Daejeon, South Korea, and a bartender in London. Even when they were technically split up, Layton would email Candace every day or two, wherever he was in the world. He never dated anyone else on those travels—it's not that he didn't want to be with her, but he needed to do all these other things on his own first. Candace was certain that after he got it all out of his system, he'd be ready for the sort of grown-up relationship she craved. She always returned to Layton because after a period of absence, he'd pull some knee-weakening romantic gesture—or at least so seeming for an infatuated young woman. He torrented songs to make CDs for her that they'd blast on weekend road trips: "Slow Mix 2000" and "L8N's ROCHESTER ROAD TUNES 2K.2," filled with Top 40 hits from the likes of Swollen Members, Britney Spears, and Usher. One summer, when he was twenty, he took a job working at a camp in New York and made Candace a custom alphabet book.

> A: You have a really nice ASS, hey what a romantic word
> to start off with, but it is definitely one of your assets
> (maybe you should put it on your resume)
> . . .
> J: Because you're cool when my drunk-ass gets JEALOUS
> about those scummy losers hitting on you downtown
> . . .
> M: The way you MELT in my arms after we make love.

When Candace would bring up marriage, Layton would rib her. "Who are you marrying?" he'd ask. But after years of breakups and reconciliations, by 2010 it seemed like Candace had finally gotten something resembling a long-term commitment out of Layton.

Layton had been taking interior design and then photography classes in Montreal while Candace had begun work as a dietitian in Ottawa, just two hours away. In photography school, he cajoled Candace into posing for sexy photos: her chest pressed up against Plexiglas, sporting a too-tight white buttoned shirt and tie, her deep jade eyes staring lustily at the camera (before cracking up as soon as the shutter clicked). Eventually, he moved in with her in Ottawa as he began work as a wedding photographer, mostly as an assistant. But Layton still felt wanderlust.

The compromise was that they would make a big leap together: to Australia. Candace, who needed some career direction, had enrolled in an eighteen-month nursing program at an Australian university and had paid her thirty-thousand-dollar deposit. The plan was that she'd move there first and start school; after Layton wrapped up the season of shooting weddings, he'd join her. It was the best of both worlds for Layton: he would permanently escape the cold, dark winters of Halifax and have his favourite person with him. He was done with the excruciating loneliness that came with travelling on his own. At one point during his time in South Korea, Layton was invited over for dinner by a local—a much-needed social invitation to break him out of his feeling of extreme isolation—but when he arrived at his new acquaintance's home, he quickly learned he'd been befriended only because this person was desperate to have someone to practise their English with.

Layton's relationship with Candace was his second one ever. It had to mean something that after all these years and all these trips, Candace had stuck with him and he still wanted to be with her.

Candace, whose obsession with organizing went back to childhood, had made lists of what to apply for, what to pack, and what to sell, and had mapped out a schedule that counted down to their departure. Their apartment in The Glebe neighbourhood in Ottawa had been emptied: they'd sold off nearly everything they owned except their pots and pans and their bed.

But in the background of all this was the mole. Candace hadn't noticed it, but Layton had a habit of studying it in the steamed-up mirror after he got out of the shower. It was 2.2 millimetres wide and looked like a tiny shrimp with its head still attached. Many blemishes dotted Layton's back, but this one, just between his spine and left shoulder blade, stood out because it was pink in a constellation of brown spots.

In March 2010, months before their planned move to Australia, the mole started bleeding, and Layton went to a walk-in clinic one day when Candace was at work and a doctor removed it. He returned and four more suspicious moles were excised from his back, leaving behind a topography of craters that bled through his white T-shirts. He didn't let Candace hug him for weeks because his skin was so raw. Sometimes, he was woken up by the pain and would slip out of bed while Candace was asleep and sit on the toilet in the bathroom, quietly tormented. He didn't tell her what was going on, convinced it would cause unnecessary worry just before their big move. The sneaking around made him feel like he was cheating, but he knew it was worth it because soon he'd get the all-clear and he could pretend this had never happened.

In May, Layton learned the first mole had been sent to a lab and had tested positive for melanoma. He was given a pamphlet with survivability statistics for each stage—how long, on average, you could expect to live from the point of diagnosis. There was nothing past ten years. It was so unexpected. As soon as he read it, he wished he could travel back in time, just thirty seconds earlier, and have that information scrubbed from his brain.

How had this happened to Layton? It seemed pretty clear to him. Of all the trips he'd done, the stint in Manly Beach, Australia, was his favourite because of the long hours he got to spend in the sun. It was one of the main reasons he and Candace had decided to make the move there.

Layton had worked at a deli from 2 to 9 p.m. daily, which freed up mornings and early afternoons for jogging along the beach, snorkelling, or lounging on the sand—and rarely with any sunscreen on. He loved tanning beds, too—drawn to them in part by vanity, but mostly because he was addicted to being warm. He loved the feeling of those UV rays on his skin, the way his always-cold toes and fingers felt blanketed by warmth. How he could feel the sun lightening each hair on his arms, evenly turning all his exposed skin golden.

Weeks passed following his diagnosis, and one Friday evening when Candace returned from work, Layton told her they had to talk. His tone made her nervous. They were standing in their gutted apartment, ahead of a life-changing move that they'd been planning for two years, and she was convinced he was going to break up with her.

Instead, he confessed he'd been diagnosed with cancer and needed surgery to remove some lymph nodes. He wasn't even going to tell her—he hoped to secretly have the surgery and then move to Australia as planned—but his business partner at the time had warned him that he would tell Candace if Layton didn't.

As the news reached Candace's ears, she felt the floor open up under her. All she wanted to do in that moment was talk it through with Layton, but there wasn't an opportunity for that. After dropping this life-changing update in her lap, he left, as he had scheduled an engagement shoot for that evening.

Later, in June, when Layton was in surgery, Candace sat in the waiting area. She'd told her parents but had otherwise kept mum about what was going on with her boyfriend. *If I don't tell anybody, it's not true*, she thought. Layton would have his surgery, have a quick recovery, and then they'd get the all-clear to go to Australia. Like Layton, Candace chose to view this cancer surgery as a minor setback.

Layton still maintained some of his wedding gigs after the surgery—he felt he had the strength to do them, but more importantly, how could he bail on clients at the last minute? At one June wedding, Candace drove him to the venue and sat in the car all day waiting for him to finish so she could take him home—the doctors had advised him not to get behind the wheel for some time.

The all-clear Layton and Candace were waiting for never came. The team at the cancer clinic told Layton they'd found some cancerous cells in the sentinel node, which sends out signals to all the "baby" nodes. It was through these nodes that the cancer could spread widely through his body. The plan was to do a second surgery to remove as many nodes as possible from under Layton's armpits. This was serious, they told him. The cancer was at Stage 3A. Layton called Candace, who was visiting her parents in Prince Edward Island, on video chat to tell her. The trip to Australia was cancelled. Candace got a refund on her tuition deposit. It was time for Layton to tell his parents.

On a June evening, the phone rang in one of the bedrooms upstairs at Layton's parents' house in Halifax, where Willie, his mother, was getting ready for a night out. Willie was the sort of mom who was both a doer and a feeler, with narrow, rounded shoulders that would envelop you in a warm but efficient hug before she set forth on the task at hand. Part of her career was spent as principal at an inner-city school where she believed arts programming could transform the lives of the most disadvantaged children. Before that, she'd been a social worker involved with foster care. Now, she worked at an art gallery and was preparing for a carnival-themed fundraiser— her outfit, a jester's costume, was laid out on the bed. She picked up the receiver and was delighted to hear her son's voice. It had been a while. She'd come to expect no more than three-line emails from him these days.

"Oh hey, thought I'd give you a call, Mum," Layton said. "Little health scare."

"Oh?" she asked, the smile disappearing from her face.

"I had a mole on my back and I had it removed."

As she tried to listen to her son, a little voice began repeating the same line again and again in Willie's head: *It's not just a mole. It's not just a mole. It's not just a mole.*

He explained the sequence of events, trying to downplay them. He told her he was going to have another surgery.

"I'm coming out," Willie blurted.

"You don't have to, Mum," Layton said.

"I'm coming," she said, adamant, trying to steady her voice.

"Okay, I just want to say one thing: don't go to the computer and start looking this stuff up," he said.

She promised she wouldn't. She knew her son's fate without having to go to the computer. If he was having a few hundred lymph nodes removed, this was cancer that could spread to the rest of his body—that maybe already had. She went down the stairs to tell Phil, her tall, bespectacled, and reserved husband, and they sank into silence together. And then, breaking her promise to Layton, Willie began her internet research.

∙

When Willie arrived in Ottawa at the end of June, ahead of Layton's surgery, Candace was relieved. Knowing Willie was there to take control of the situation meant Candace could crumble. There was a comfort that came from having a mom—any mom, really—around.

Before he went into the operating room, Layton sent Willie an email, informing her of a secret plan: "mum, I'm going to ask candace to marry me. yeah, i know." It was as though he could hear his mother saying, "Oh really? Good timing, darling."

When it came to the proposal, Layton knew he needed Candace's mother, Irma, on his side, too. Candace and Irma were incredibly close: back when Candace lived in the same city as her parents, she'd go grocery shopping with her mom, or they'd go for runs in the park, even after she'd moved out with her friends.

Irma always liked Layton, and thought he had a real romantic side to him. The summer Layton worked at camp and sent Candace—then living at her parents' house—dozens of love letters in the mail, Candace's father, Kerry, would grumble about his daughter's boyfriend making him look bad.

But when Layton was travelling, Irma thought he was too independent and might never settle down. When they announced plans to move to Australia, she was delighted: maybe they'd get married there and start a family.

Layton sent an email to Irma. He wanted to ask Candace to marry him and asked whether she was okay with it. "Yes, of course," Irma replied. She was aware of Layton's cancer but had raised her daughter not to abandon someone when they had a setback. Now was the test.

Layton had no money for a diamond and asked Willie if his grandmother had left behind any rings. She had a cameo pin, and Layton figured he could eventually make that Candace's wedding ring. After his second surgery, he was wheeled to a recovery room and asked a nurse to fetch Candace because he needed her help with something. When Candace arrived, he proposed on bended knee.

Candace had wanted to get married for a long time. She knew Layton was the person she was supposed to be with. *If he has cancer, I'll take him with cancer*, she thought, and said yes. But as the day wore on, she kept asking him if he was sure. If he had just proposed because he felt guilty about their trip to Australia being sidelined. "No," he said. "I really want this."

In July, several doctor's appointments later, Layton started on Interferon, a drug administered like chemotherapy but used to boost the body's immune system to help it fight cancer. He was told there was only a 10 per cent chance the drug would be effective at purging his body of the disease, but it was presented as the best option.

On that first night of the initial three-week treatment cycle, Layton's temperature soared to 104 degrees and he was taken to emergency. As he lay in a hospital hallway, his body convulsed so violently it shook the whole bed. Some mornings he'd wake up to get treatment, then come back to bed and not rise again until the next morning. His skin would be freezing cold one minute and he'd be an uncomfortable, sweating mess the next. Forget the cancer, it was the drug he worried about surviving.

As Layton went through treatment, he and Candace spent long days like John and Yoko in their bedroom. They'd sometimes have entire conversations in the imagined voices of the neighbourhood stray cats. While Layton slept, Candace alternated between numbing her brain with *Sex and the City* DVDs and checking out books and documentaries on cancer survivors from the public library. She made it a daily ritual to take head-clearing two-hour bike rides along the Rideau Canal.

For a few years, Candace and Layton had had a joint bank account that had served as a travel fund—they both threw money in there when they could, with the plan to pay for spontaneous trips. But now, with neither of them working, they quickly drained the account to pay for living expenses.

In September, partway through the four months of treatment, Layton and Candace moved back to Halifax to be near Layton's family. When she'd moved to Ottawa, Candace had bought a 2007 Volkswagen Jetta in Halifax and driven it to her new home. Now she packed up her possessions and Layton's and drove back to her hometown.

They planned their wedding in three months and got married in a little venue called The Music Room. Their invitations were sent out to a small number of friends and family, featuring a repeating grid of a goofy portrait-studio photo of the two dressed as yuppie yacht owners: crisp white shirts buttoned all the way to the top, with sweaters loosely knotted around their necks, their mouths wide but eyes dead, like ventriloquists' dummies.

> *candace & layton*
> *are getting hitched!*
> *oct 2nd, 2010*
>
> *join our*
> *super sexy*
> *super sweet*
> *wedding day!*

On the big day, Layton was in a white shirt and his one pair of black dress pants—both worn a little loose—with a pair of black suspenders strapped over his shoulders. He had a black bow tie and a white gerbera daisy tucked into the pocket of his jacket. He looked handsome, but more like an eighteen-year-old at prom than a groom on his wedding day. Candace was a more elegant version of her everyday self: her hair was in a loose updo to show off her pearl drop earrings and she wore a strapless satin wedding gown that gave her an hour-glass figure.

It felt like the longest two minutes of his life while Layton stood waiting for Candace to walk down the aisle in front of everyone as Greg Laswell's cover of Kate Bush's "This Woman's Work" played. When they faced each other for the brief ceremony, they beamed, like dimples had been permanently carved into their cheeks.

Layton, as serious as he'd ever been, read his vows.

It's 7 pm. A chilly fall evening. It's getting darker earlier these days.

We're moving boxes into our new apartment in Halifax. And you're so excited. We're in the kitchen, and like a child you're dancing wildly to Grease songs and I'm trying my best to keep up. We might look awkward but by god if we can't dance.

I take a minute to soak it all in. To think about the last ten years. The last ten weeks.

I look at you now and you just seem so . . . happy. Happy to be home. Happy to be in a new apartment, and for whatever reason, happy to be marrying me.

I think about the day I got the call from the doctor and that night we skyped from PEI and how you dropped two years of planning to come and take care of me and I think about me huddled on the floor in that hospital stall with my powder blue gown and grannie's ring . . . and all of it, the whole experience . . . makes me smile. Because like you always say . . . "everything happens for a reason."

And this time you were right.

Cause in a few days we're getting married. We'll sign papers, we'll eat cake, and we'll be surrounded by everyone we love.

It'll be perfect.

And the next day when the dust settles and everyone has gone home we'll be alone again.

But we'll have each other.

And whatever happens from here on in, we'll face it together.

I'll be burning the midnight oil and you'll be up at the crack of dawn. I'll be drinking green juices and you'll be making homemade kale chips. I'll complain about the taste and you'll tell me to shut up and eat them anyway.

You will save my life. And I will owe you mine.

And nothing will stand in our way. Cause yup. We're in love.

Today. Tomorrow. Forever.

•

After the wedding, Layton and Candace drove an hour north of Halifax to the tiny town of Shortts Lake, for a minimoon.

They'd been loaned a family friend's cabin for a few days. It was rustic: no electricity, no reliable running water. A sign in the bathroom told them to keep their showers to sixty seconds. Candace was the first to try it out. She stripped down, stepped underneath the shower head, turned on the faucet and faced her new husband. "Okay, Layton, count." He only got up to "ten Mississippi" when the water shut off. They shrieked with laughter and Layton towelled her off. They stood at the short dock to watch the sunset, they played Monopoly, they ate carrot and celery sticks by the light of a pillar candle balanced in an egg cup.

Before they'd completed a month as newlyweds, Layton stopped taking Interferon—earlier than his doctors had wanted, because of how scary the side effects had become. Slowly, Layton's body recovered, his energy and endurance returned, and he was able to step back into comforting old patterns. He and Candace could go for walks again, grab lunch together, and Layton could even indulge in a Philly cheese-steak without Candace scolding him about its sodium and fat content (though she still insisted he glug down green juices to boost his health). In the months that followed, a series of CT scans and chest X-rays showed no traces of the disease in his body. He was Layton the photographer and the husband now, not just Layton the cancer patient. Things finally seemed normal. Not every cough made him paranoid. Indigestion was just indigestion.

Now that Layton seemed healthy, Candace had a new worry. She'd always had the deep-seated fear of him leaving: *When's he going to take off again for another trip?* In the past, he'd always sprung it on her with little notice. *Shit, he's going to get tired of this and go away for a while*, she thought now. But it didn't happen.

That winter, Layton surprised Candace with a trip to an all-inclusive in Mexico—the opposite of his ideal vacation but a break the two badly needed to celebrate surviving the year. For the first time in his life, he slathered on sunscreen each morning, reapplying it judiciously every few hours. The room at their resort was stocked with cans of Coca-Cola and bags of potato chips, but those were a no-go. Some of the books Candace had read during Layton's Interferon days were about people who had done alternative therapies to treat their cancer, and now that he was feeling better, she convinced him to start eating cleaner. Out with the junk food and empty calories and in with the whole grains, vegetables, and sludgy green juices, which Candace mixed in their hotel room with the handle of a toothbrush. Back at home after Mexico, though, Layton would sometimes sneak away to his room and put a bit of ketchup on one of the meals Candace had prepared, or relish the rubbery chicken breast he was served at the weddings he went to shoot. This was not hitchhiking through Brazil or stumbling into pubs in England, but it was a shared life, and one whose benefits he was beginning to appreciate.

•

Layton and Candace had been living in a basement apartment since they returned to Halifax. Candace had found a job processing short-term disability claims with a health insurance provider, but she wanted a family and the next step for her was a house. Layton fought her bitterly on it—a house? With their income? What if he stayed better for a long time—permanently, even? Now they were just going to be anchored to Halifax forever? But Candace knew how to make the pitch. She wasn't going to drag him out to some characterless subdivision with tidy cul-de-sacs and the sort of homes you could win in a hospital fundraiser. They could find something small and charming and affordable in the heart of the city. Maybe in a few years, when they had some more money, they could do some renovations—really turn it into Layton's dream home.

Something pretty close to the fantasy presented itself to them in a Craigslist ad. It was a tiny place, just 1,305 square feet, on a lot five times its size bordered by a thick tangle of trees. There were two bedrooms, a bathroom, and a small kitchen with just enough space for two people to sit and eat. It was close to a pond, a park they both already loved, and just down the road from the community theatre where Layton's father, Phil, volunteered. "Skating & snowshoeing in the winter; hiking & water activities in the summer," the listing bragged. It was as Layton-friendly as a house could be and just a short drive from Candace's work.

When they moved in, the house, which had been used as a cottage, was filled with the sort of castoff seating that furnishes university students' first apartments. They threw it all out and ordered a massive sectional sofa that filled the living room. Layton had a knack for making places feel homey quickly—even if he wasn't going to live in them for long. In a summer rental he got with Candace in their early days of dating, he hung art and filled the space with houseplants. This time he bought clever screenprints and framed them and mounted photos of him and Candace from their goofy engagement shoot and others from their wedding day. He painted the doors pumpkin and the stair risers yellow and white.

It was strange to have spent his twenties running from the grown-up life in Halifax he'd seen so many of his childhood friends embrace and then to find himself back here living it himself, albeit a little delayed. Just two years earlier, he'd wanted to try living in Montreal without an apartment as a fun experiment. Now he, Layton Reid, was a homeowner.

Dear house:

Eight months here man, what a trip.

It seems like just yesterday I first laid eyes on you.
It's safe to say I'm more in love with you now than ever.

Like most good things in my life I was kind of forced into making the commitment to own you. Kind of like marrying my wife. Candace wanted to buy a house so bad but you know me man I just wasn't ready. I've got commitment issues, we all know that. Every morning she'd scour Viewpoint looking for houses she could see us settling into and would show me the listings and I'd walk out of the room rolling my eyes, murmuring . . . meh . . . under my breath.

Until the day she found you. Our diamond in the rough.
Our perfect fit.

You were a little cottage house tucked away in a well-treed lot in a village-like neighbourhood called Jollimore, and the second I drove up the driveway to see if the chemistry was there it was love at first sight. Well, no one was home so we had to like climb through the bushes and peek into the house like creepy pedophiles but yeah, I wanted a piece of that real bad.

There was no way around it. It was you or no house at all.

So we marched into the bank with nothing more than a stack of wedding contracts and a handful of laundered 100 dollar bills and walked out with keys in hand. First-time homeowners, shit. Scary stuff. It took some time to get used to your wood stove, but we're damn near pros now. You've got more charm than you know what to do with I tell you. Some nights I sit outside in the dark and listen to the peepers in the pond next door and just kind of look at you. Not like in a weird way. Just admiring. I've spent so much of my life living out of a suitcase moving from one place to the next it's the first time in a long time I've actually been proud of something I own.

Well, besides Candace.

I know you're old, something like eighty-years-old, but man you've aged well. You're close to the Dingle and the Frog Pond and William's Lake and mom loves working in the garden and we've got quirky neighbours and deer in the backyard and lots of natural light and privacy and we're so damn comfortable here you're going to have to just bury us all in the backyard when we kick the bucket. Me, the wife, Gracie, Callie and our soccer team of ghost babies, every one. It'll probably be years before we have the inside looking just perfect, but I promise you won't lose that cottage vibe we fell for in the beginning, or replace you with stainless-steel-granite-bacon-wrapped-scallop-countertops, or any of that nonsense.

Let's be honest, we're still filling in dents in the furniture with magic marker.

So yeah, we love you just the way you are. Perfectly imperfect.

Thanks for having us, house.

Let's get old together, ok?

.

Maybe it felt natural to put down roots in his hometown because, for the first time, he'd found something that could be a proper career, something he could do for decades, not just some joe job he took so he could get money to pay his rent or cover his next flight out. Photography made sense as a pursuit for someone as naturally curious and prone to boredom as Layton. It was equal parts control and chaos. It was surreal to him that people would pay money—and so much money—just to have him tag along on their wedding day to take pictures. He was so bothered by that, in fact, that he couldn't bring himself to charge anywhere close to what many others in the city did, something that attracted constant scolding from his friendly competitors.

Matt, his older brother, had studied photography while away at university but found he had trouble connecting to his subjects, even simply remembering their names. It irritated him that Layton had a natural gift for putting people at ease. It was strange for Matt to observe his brother in this new light: here was something he was passionate about and truly gifted at. He'd noticed the quality of his brother's work when Layton kept a travel blog and could see it really mature when he started taking photos professionally.

Layton preferred to meet couples for coffee before contracts were signed—they could see if they liked him and,
more importantly, he could see if he liked them. If he met
with an interested couple at a coffee shop and observed them
bickering a lot or noticed the groom-to-be was constantly
checking his phone, Layton would email them later to say he
was already booked for the weekend in question. He wanted
to feel invested in the couples he was photographing—he
wanted to believe they were going to make it. Sometimes, it
was only on the wedding day he would learn his café assess-
ments of people weren't always the most accurate. He'd be
trying to find a delicate way to tell a couple to make their
embrace seem more sincere, or to smile at each other in a way
that suggested they didn't despise each other and think, *Oh
God, I feel terrible for these people.* It was nice at the end of one
of those marathon days to drive in the inky night down the
quiet roads to his little butter-coloured house that felt especially like a cottage in the summer. He'd crawl into bed with
Candace and be thankful for his marriage, which seemed so
simple and easy.

But Candace wasn't quite so satisfied. Layton had fought
hard against all the traditional things she wanted—having
children most of all. In the period after their final breakup,
when they were thinking about getting back together for the
long haul, Candace was firm about one thing: having kids had
to be an option.

"Okay," Layton said. "I'm not promising plural, though."

That was enough for Candace. Soon after they were married, she started nudging Layton. She wanted a dog, she said,

and eventually he agreed and they got Gracie, an American Staffordshire mix. She was lean, with muscular legs and a coat of paprika-coloured fur. On one of their first weeks with Gracie, they took her out to a cottage for a weekend where a massive, very aggressive dog seemed to be obsessed with their new puppy. Protecting their new pet and choosing which drinks to buy at the liquor store were the biggest concerns they had for the whole weekend. It dawned on Layton that, for the first time in a while, there were no stresses in their lives. Cancer was in the rear-view mirror.

In this newly relaxed state, Layton grew to enjoy, or at least tolerate, Gracie. The first year with her, he worked from home, and on weekdays he'd take her out for walks. But he soon regretted saying yes; he'd thought allowing a dog would satisfy Candace's maternal urges, but now all she could talk about was how nice it would be to have a baby. And like she had done before, she wore Layton down.

Layton thought of this logically. He loved Candace, right? He wanted to be with her for the rest of his life, right? And giving her what she wanted would make her happy, right? He wasn't comfortable with the idea of having a child, but he reluctantly agreed to try.

In late October 2012, Candace and Layton flew to New York for a quick vacation, scheduled around his birthday. Their plans were upended by Hurricane Sandy, which killed at least 233 people as it cut a path northward from the Caribbean Sea. Stranded in a motel, what else was there for them to do but try to make a baby? Candace, who tracked her period on an app on her phone, knew that the window during which she ovulated each month would come up on this trip. She assumed this would be the first month of many where they tried to make a baby—she had friends who'd had lots of trouble, so she figured it might be two years before she got pregnant. Each time after she and Layton had sex, she'd do a headstand, joking that this would help his sperm swim up to meet her egg.

Along with many others in New York and New Jersey that weekend, Candace and Layton conceived a Hurricane Sandy baby. When they got back to Halifax and learned they were expecting, Layton was almost a little disappointed at how quickly it had happened—he'd expected the upside of this deal was a multi-month sex marathon. He opened a document on his computer the day he learned he'd be a father, eager to talk to a child—his child—who was then just a cluster of cells.

well shit little nugget. i guess i'll call you nugget for now. ghost baby doesn't have the same ring to it. candace, that's your mom btw came home from work today with a little stick and a plus sign on it. she peeked into the spare room where i was sneaking some lunch i had put ketchup on to mask the . . . well she cooks clean, you'll see what i mean later. then she slipped back out of the room after a quick hug like she'd told me what she bought at the grocery store.

to be honest when she told me my first reaction was oh brother, that's literally what i was thinking, and i'm pretty sure that came out of my mouth. mostly shock i guess. she says we have to get a blood test to make sure it's all legit but yeah. crazy. she'd been pestering me for like a year and two weeks of trying and BAM. what can i say. apart from feeling

in shock i got this weird rush of calm fall over me as i went
into the bathroom alone. i don't know what that meant.
i went downstairs and put on my sneakers, she wanted to go
for a walk in the park with gracie and i'm trying to get back
into running. i just looked at her like, are we gonna even talk
about this (your mom's a talker and not normally quiet about
this kind of stuff). she said she was in shock in the morning
but started to get this excited feeling as the day wore on. it's
10 o'clock now, we just watched a movie, limitless (meh) and
now i'm working on my last wedding of the season. i don't
know how i'm going to feel about this in the morning but for
now . . . i don't know. i feel different. excited? what's another
word for excited. anxious? looking forward to seeing where
all this goes. either way, i love you. good night.

.

When he was ready to tell Willie and Phil they were going to
be grandparents, Layton explained he was working on a new
project that involved word association and portraiture. He
started throwing out words and taking photos of his parents
as they replied with the first word that came to mind.

"Candace," he said, clicking down his shutter.

His mother's face softened and she tilted her head to the
side. "Sweet," she said, smiling at her daughter-in-law.

"Pregnant," Layton said and Phil immediately jumped up
from the couch to hug Layton and Candace. It took Willie a
few seconds to process the information, but she soon joined in
the celebration.

Phil had always felt a little guilty about how happy he was to have his son back in Halifax. Matt, his eldest, was here now too, but he'd gone through the loss of his boys so many times already—when they went away to school, on all of Layton's travels. But then Layton got sick and he came home. It was kind of a gift. And now, even better, Layton was going to give him a grandchild.

week 12. today we went to the doctor's and they used some thing to check for your heartbeat and after a bit of tinkering bang there it was your little super fast alien beating heart. i guess you're the size of a peach now, that's kind of crazy. we're told after 12 weeks there's a better chance that you'll live . . . i guess a lot of babies don't make it that far along . . . soo, congrats on that. it's also kind of the reason i think it took so long to write this . . . just in case you know, you weren't up for sticking around. what can i say your mom is a worrier. anyway, at the office i took video with this really easy to use but shitty quality flip video that you'll most likely make fun of when you're older because it will be so archaic-looking but documenting all this is really important to me and i hope someday you'll look back and feel the same way . . . your world is gonna look a lot different than the one we were raised in but that's not such a bad thing. your mom has been feeling pretty shit lately mostly due to you actually growing inside her, and on top of that she got a shitty cold. they tell us she'll start feeling better after the first three months so i think things will start to get back to a little more normal in the coming weeks. for now we've only told our

parents (you'll meet them soon enough) and my brother
and a select few friends. tomorrow i'll likely have to put it
online so everyone knows at the same time. to be honest
i'm not really sure how i feel about that. you don't know
this yet but someday you're gonna hear a band you love
so much and you'll be hesitating to share them because you
feel like . . . such a strong connection that it doesn't feel
right. that's kind of how i feel about you tonight. we're at
the stage where we really have to start thinking about how
to accommodate a little alien baby in our house and make
you comfortable and keep you alive for as long as it takes
for you to stay alive on your own. that's heavy stuff to think
about. we bought a little house in a neighbourhood you're
going to make so many great memories in but for now your
room is pretty much empty. and i've been using the closet.
i don't mind sharing though. the walls were meant to be grey
but turned out blue so i'm not sure what's going to happen
there. i'm half tempted to paint the walls a neon pink if
you're a boy in honour of your grandma but i'll fill you in on
what she and dad taught me sometime when you're a little
older. boy or girl we're happy you're happy to stay for now.
i love you. good night.

.

When they learned that they were having a son, Layton was
ecstatic. At the doctor's appointment, he brought his video
camera to film the moment but was so overcome with emotion he forgot to hit record. The prospect of parenthood felt

absurd much of the time to Layton. At a prenatal instructional session in the spring, Layton and Candace were the bad kids in the back of the class, laughing so hard during a nursing video of a woman pushing her breast into her infant's face that they were unable to breathe.

ok dude we're now at the six-and-a-half-month mark, crazy. and i haven't written down a thing, terrible father. you probably already know this by now but you're a boy. yeah man! i didn't care either way but now that we know it seems somehow like a relief. your mom has been feeling pretty good lately, a lot better than the last time we talked. she has trouble sleeping now and then since her stomach is so massive but all in all you're pretty good to her. moving around and doing side-kicks, it's great. i actually felt you kicking a few weeks back which was pretty incredible. your room is coming along pretty nicely, we hope you like it. it's decked out with a crib and dresser and some clothes people have been giving us. LOTS of clothes people have been giving us. everyone seems to be having boys lately so that definitely will work in our favour. i forgot to mention the ultrasound. they're really mean and don't let you take pictures or video during the whole thing but we did get to see a bunch of angles of you that looked a little blurry but we were happy nonetheless that you seemed to be happy/ healthy. no idea what we were looking at but couldn't stop smiling. a good friend of mine called yesterday to tell me they had a miscarriage which is when the baby doesn't make it long enough to come out of the mom, which was really

sad. that actually happens a lot more than you'd think. so
obviously we're stoked you're sticking around for now and
can't wait to meet you in a few months — terrifying but
exciting! oh another amazing thing i've got candace on is
your nickname. there's this movie called austin powers and
he has a sidekick who is played by a little person and he
nicknames the little guy tripod because his wiener is so big
it looks like a tripod you know? aaaanyway, it's awesome
because your mom calls you trip now for short which i find
highly amusing. your for real name on the other hand is
going to be a challenge. do you know how many terrible
boys' names there are out there? it's tough man, thinking of
one that will suit you. i wish i could just ask you what you
wanted to be called. you'd probably come up with something
amazing like razcan or something, on account of you not
being in this world just yet. it'll probably be something
simple, your mom has had a lot of really bad name ideas for
you so far but luckily i usually have the final say on these
kinds of things. she means well, but you're def not going to
be called hunter, or mason, or any of the other terrible and
trendy names floating around. i really wanted to call you
will after your great grandpa (you'll hear about him a little
later on) but mom put the kibosh on that. she thinks it's
too close to my mom's and brother's names (wilma and
william). i still like it, simple, strong, not too masculine,
or intimidating. whatever we call you you'll be killer. talk
to you in a few trip. we love you.

.

It had been so long that he'd been healthy that, in the spring of 2013, when Layton started to get bad stomach pains that would come and go every three weeks, he assumed it was nothing serious. One night while he and Candace were out for a walk at York Redoubt, a nearby park, he complained about the pain and Candace suggested he go see his family doctor—it was probably just an ulcer, she told him. Layton went for an appointment while Candace, then near the end of her second trimester and exhausted, stayed home.

The timing of Layton's appointment was fortuitous: his family doctor had received the results of his latest scan before an oncologist had the chance to call Layton. He laid it all out: the melanoma had resurfaced in a bad way. Layton had a tumour on his left lung and another on his stomach. This meant his cancer was now at Stage IV, the most advanced stage, when the majority of patients can expect to live a few years at best.

His head filled with static, Layton detoured to his parents' place instead of driving home. He climbed the stairs to the den and told them the news. The three sat in silence for what felt like several minutes. And then Layton cleared his throat, jumping to the conclusion he knew everyone in the room had already drawn but nobody wanted to say aloud: soon he'd be dead.

"Okay, so Candace and the baby can stay here, right?" he asked.

•

When Layton arrived back at his own house, he walked into the living room where Candace was sitting on the couch in the same place Gracie often liked to lie. Layton stood a few feet away by the back door, uncharacteristically solemn.

"How'd it go?" Candace asked.

"Oh, you know, he thinks it's reflux and gave me these," he said, holding up some pills he'd picked up at the pharmacy. He paused. "But the rest isn't so good."

"What do you mean?" Candace asked.

He'd already had some practice in wording this and laid it all out, quickly, simply. "Yeah, it came back," he said.

As she absorbed the news, everything in her body sank. She began shaking and felt a wave of nausea. This was catastrophic. But she knew that if she was really stressed, it might force her body into early labour and little Trip wasn't ready to come out yet—he was only twenty-three weeks along. She had to be calm. They were already dealing with a crisis and didn't need another.

The house suddenly felt claustrophobic. They went for a walk around the neighbourhood, mostly in silence. While each of them needed to mentally process this on their own, they also needed the comfort of proximity to each other.

As a teenager who didn't know any better, Layton once got together with friends on a Friday night and poured an ounce of each kind of booze the group could rustle up from their parents' liquor cabinets into a big cooler with a spout on the side. They consumed all of the disgusting concoction and passed out. When Layton woke up, he vomited on himself. He learned after that to take it easy—when his friends drank hard in the early evening to pre-game before going out to a bar, Layton would only start at 9 p.m., usually just nursing a single beer, afraid he might overdo it. He hadn't had a drink in a while, but that night, after he and Candace returned home, he thought it was the right time for a beer. He sipped it slowly and thoughtfully, wondering if it might be one of his last.

·

The next morning, Candace called her mother, sobbing, with the news, catching her just before she left for work. Irma was worried for her son-in-law, but immediately thought about the child her daughter was carrying and started crying too, much to Candace's annoyance.

"No, you're not allowed to be upset! I'm upset and you need to be here for me," she chided.

Candace sent her boss an email telling her she would need a few days off to process things. Between her and Layton, she'd always been the hypochondriac, self-diagnosing non-existent illnesses and allergies. Layton would always be the one to reassure her she was fine.

"I'm going to be the one that something's going to happen to," he'd tell her. "I'm gonna get cancer. One of us is going to get cancer, because everybody gets cancer. There's no escaping it, really." And he was right.

He'd navigated danger and dodged death so many times during his adventures that having his lights turned out by cancer seemed rather unpoetic. In South Africa, he'd been knifed and knocked out by a mugger, he'd been deported from South Korea, he contracted some mysterious tropical illness in Brazil that caused him to pass out in the bathroom on the plane ride home. The first year they were in their new house, Layton, channelling his Dennis the Menace childhood self, wanted Candace to take a picture of him doing a stupid stunt jumping off a swing set and he broke his collarbone. The next year, he got into a collision on the highway and totalled his parents' car.

His accident-prone nature went back to childhood. When he learned to ride a bike on the street he grew up on, his mother and father took turns holding on to the seat as he pedalled and then let go. Overconfident Layton crashed into a thornbush on his first few tries. A few weeks later, while recklessly zig-zagging down the street, he collided with a neighbour's car. He was tilting back in a chair once and hit his head on a radiator. He smashed his head on a different radiator at a friend's house when he fell down the stairs. He dressed up as Peter Pan once for Halloween and carried around a real knife through the night. While picking food out from between two teeth with it, he chipped a tooth. He so routinely visited the emergency room that on one trip a child protection worker took him aside for questioning, concerned his parents were abusing him.

Now he was a frequent flyer in the hospital once more.

Of all the places in this building, he most hated the hallway he was rolled down before the surgery to remove the tumour in his stomach, a smooth, grey-tan bulbous growth nearly three centimetres wide. That hallway felt like a morgue to him: it was cold, sterile, and dark save for the severe glow of overhead fluorescent lights. No surgeon wanted to touch the tumour on Layton's lung—it was too close to many veins and arteries—so only the stomach one would come out for now.

Sometimes, after having a really sweet interaction with one of the nurses, Layton vowed that when he got better, he'd volunteer at the hospital to say thanks. But then he'd briefly feel healthy and wonder what in the hell he'd been thinking. When he was well, he didn't want anything to do with this space that symbolized death and dying and disease.

Dr. Davis was figuring out the limits to what Layton wanted to know and he was doing the same. At one appointment, she mentioned the size of the tumour on his lung and he let her discuss it because he figured he needed that information. But as soon as she said, "Let's take a look at it on the screen" and was about to project his chest X-ray, he panicked. "No, I'm not interested," he said.

A social worker met with Layton and asked if there was any help he needed. She offered Candace and him a stack of coupons for half-off parking in the hospital lot—a slap in the face, as Layton saw it. *I'm afraid you have terminal cancer. Here, have some parking passes. It's literally the least we can do.* He mentioned how he was stressed about work, how he was self-employed and wasn't sure what this meant for the household finances. The social worker gave him an application for a government terminal disability benefit. He couldn't even focus on how much money he might collect each month through this benefit because he was too stuck on the name. It was the first time he and Candace had been so aggressively confronted with that word: terminal. *You can't just give out forms like that to people,* Candace thought. *Maybe if you were eighty you could process what it meant, but to give a form like that to a man in his thirties?*

The social worker could see their faces change as they fixated on that word. "Yeah, it's a bad name," she said apologetically.

Once they got home, Candace and Layton had a hearty cry as it dawned on them that if the government was going to shell out $850 a month as part of this benefit, clearly they didn't think Layton would be around long enough to break the bank.

Money was on everyone's mind now. Candace held her breath waiting to hear if Layton's treatment would be covered by the critical illness insurance she'd bought a few years earlier—he'd already faced that first stretch of cancer before she'd purchased it and she worried he might not be covered because this was a pre-existing condition. She'd bought the policy on a whim at work, worried that after a long day of shooting, Layton might get into a car accident coming home from a wedding, or that he might injure his hand in a way that compromised his ability to operate a camera.

When Candace got the call that Layton would be covered, she squealed on the phone. Layton bounded over and hugged and kissed her while she was still speaking to the agent, trying her best to sound composed.

•

Layton was due to shoot his first wedding of the 2013 season in just over a month. He'd bought a beautiful new lens for $2,000—just about what he was charging at the time to shoot a wedding. This was going to be the year he invested big time in his business, and he vowed to take only the jobs he was really passionate about. He'd booked several casual backyard celebrations. If someone got in touch about a stuffy hotel ball-room affair, he'd politely decline.

Now, with this life-changing news, he had to email the nearly two dozen couples he'd assembled in his perfect client roster, explaining his situation. He had to block half his friends on Facebook, especially those who were in the same line of work as him—it was too painful to see these snippets of their carefree lives: the new car purchases, the outdoor con-certs, the camping trips, and, of course, all the weddings they were shooting. Still, he had to beg some of them—the ones who always gave him a hard time for charging too little—to take on the gigs he had to cancel. Within two days, every couple was covered. Only one gave him a hard time about it. Another ended up booking someone who was $250 cheaper and sent Layton a card in the mail with a cheque for that amount, telling him how sorry she was about the hand he'd been dealt.

There was still one wedding Layton didn't want to cancel, though: a gig in Spain that he had booked through a former client, whose friend was now the bride-to-be. He was still recovering from his surgery, but Dr. Davis encouraged him to make the trip. When he was there, he reconnected with his old client, who pressed him about his personal life. He revealed he had cancer and she broke down in tears and then disappeared. The next time he saw her, she made him promise he wouldn't tell the bride and groom because it would put a damper on their wedding day.

The wedding was on the beach, in the blazing sun, the last place he should've been, but this was a job, maybe his last job, and he had to set his own needs aside. After the wedding, when the newlyweds exhaled and the hungover guests flew home, Layton took off for a few days to Barcelona. He wasn't interested in the Gaudi cathedral every other tourist queued up to see, or in cramming into a tapas bar at midnight for beer and a plate of *patatas bravas*. With a handful of euros in his pocket and his camera slung around his neck, he just wandered for hours, snapping photos of young couples kissing on the sidewalk, of local delivery men wheeling refrigerators down stone-paved streets, of skateboarding teens congregating on church steps.

Soon after he returned home, he stuck a pin—maybe his last—into the map on the wall, the one by illustrator Oliver Jeffers he'd lusted after for months before buying it at a discount on Black Friday. It hung in the hallway just outside the bedroom door and was dotted with pins to mark all the places he'd travelled to. But now he was no longer adding to it. When his son was born, Layton imagined he'd buy a second set of pins in another colour so the kid could also map his own voyages.

Then he went into his closet and threw out his only pair of dress pants, the one he wore to every wedding he shot. Life was too short for pleats.

•

Fewer than 20 per cent of people at Stage IV live beyond five years. There was an 80 per cent chance Layton would die before he turned forty. But no one was supposed to tell Layton that—he didn't want to know. At every turn, he avoided survivability statistics. After Layton's stomach surgery, his surgeon showed him the tumour he'd removed and it unsettled Layton in a way that was unexpected. It was a reminder that his body was a mystery to him, a vessel that could hold secrets—ones that could eventually kill him—that he wouldn't have a clue about. He didn't want to know who lived and who died, what his own odds were. It was easier to be blissfully ignorant, he decided.

After that life-and-death talk following his diagnosis, Dr. Davis offered what she thought was hopeful news: Layton tested positive for a gene mutation that made him eligible for a new pill, vemurafenib, an enzyme inhibitor that would trigger cancer cells in his body to die off. There was a 50 per cent shot the drug would work for about six months to shrink the tumour in his lung, but its effectiveness would decrease over time. She told him it wasn't a cure, but it was a good treatment. If he wanted, he could start taking it in just a few days. Candace and Layton told Dr. Davis they needed some time to think about it.

Layton, naturally, avoided reading up on it. Candace, naturally, buried herself in research. While he was taking the drug, Layton wouldn't be able to have any exposure to the sun, she read, and he could even develop secondary skin cancers. Other side effects were hair loss, rash, nausea, diarrhea, exhaustion, and headache. Most were less severe than the flu-like symptoms caused by Interferon, the drug he took last time, but for Candace and Layton, it didn't seem worth the suffering if it offered so little hope. Candace was terrified her husband would die, but she was also scared of what this drug would do to him.

She remembered how he became a different person during the previous round of treatment: sleeping all day, foggy, in physical pain. Plus, Dr. Davis said it might only work for six to eight months and then the cancer was likely to return. Was it even worth the potential misery?

Candace had done a lot of reading about nutrition and cancer during the scare in 2010, and now she was revisiting that, taking particular interest in a type of treatment that kept coming up in her searches: Gerson Therapy. It was developed in the 1930s by Max Gerson, a doctor who immigrated to the United States from Germany. He designed a diet to treat a variety of ailments, from migraines to tuberculosis to cancer.

When Layton first mentioned the therapy to me, I was skeptical. Much of what I had heard about diet as the key to fighting cancer or a number of other illnesses came in the form of irritating email forwards from my uncle with subject lines such as "Fw: God's pharmacy. This is amazing!" and "Fwd: Fw: MANIOC – My wonder drug for cancer." After researching Gerson Therapy, I learned it prescribed an organic, vegetarian diet, nutritional supplements, and fresh-squeezed juices. The treatment was based on the premise that cancer is caused by environmental toxins and electrolyte imbalances in the body. It sought to rid the body of illness through various "cleansing" practices such as frequent coffee enemas. Once the body had been cleared of pollutants, it was believed the patient's immune system would be strong enough to fight off the cancer by itself. The general logic behind the therapy made sense to Candace, who had trained to become a dietician: fill your body with the good stuff and flush out the bad.

If he tried this, Layton would be guzzling thirteen juices and giving himself five enemas daily.

Candace believed that yes, the sun exposure was the big factor that caused Layton's cancer, but there were others too, according to the Gerson Institute, which was based in San Diego. What Candace read suggested Layton was already susceptible because of his genetic predispositions. His liver couldn't handle the sun exposure in the way others' bodies could. If he strengthened his liver, maybe he could fight this. The problem was, if Layton wanted to dive into this therapy, he'd have to fly to either Mexico or Hungary to train at one of the inpatient clinics that had been licensed by the Gerson Institute—there were no clinics in Canada or the U.S. because the treatment could not be legally administered by doctors in either country.

Layton never thought he was the sort of person who would do this—he wasn't like the wheatgrass-chugging hippies or evangelical Christians whose effusive Gerson testimonials he read online. He was the guy who rolled his eyes at them, the guy who survived on Cheez Whiz sandwiches or instant ramen when travelling on a budget, who thought of food merely as calories he consumed that he would eventually burn off or part with after a trip to the bathroom.

He wondered at first if the therapy was a scam. Were the Gerson people just trying to sucker those who were ill and desperate? The institute's website promoted an entire mini-industry of Gerson-related products: training courses, videos and books, nutritional supplements, high-end juicers, and various other paraphernalia such as therapeutic coffee and T-shirts. But Candace reassured him it was a non-profit.

I couldn't help but get hung up on the fact that there was no proof—no randomized controlled studies, at any rate—that Gerson Therapy worked, save for a small bundle of research (some of it produced by the Gerson Research Organization) that is by scientific standards flawed, anecdotal, or lacking in hard statistics. But weak evidence didn't deter Gerson proponents, whose testimonials I came across online, from touting benefits of the dietary regimen they boldly claimed could "heal cancer." There were plenty of earnest bloggers out there with miraculous stories to share, and I knew as a journalist how a powerful personal story could often be more compelling than reams of lab research.

Still, these promising anecdotal accounts aside, there was the fundamental science behind cancer that couldn't be ignored. I knew it was tempting to think about cancer like an invader from without, but in fact cancer cells arise during cell division, when our DNA replicates in faulty ways. These cell clusters refuse to behave in concert with surrounding cells and seem to take on a life of their own, eventually growing into a misshapen mass of malfunctioning tissue—in Layton's case, the tumours in his lung and his stomach. There are substances like formaldehyde that are well known to cause cancer; but seemingly benign things like peppercorn and figs contain carcinogenic compounds, too. Charred barbecue meat is linked to cancer, as is not having babies and even being tall. With cancer, it sometimes seems, life is contraindicated.

I understood how for many cancer patients and the people who loved them, it could be dizzying to stay on top of what food was being touted as cancer-fighting from week to week.

Green tea and fish, yes; salt and saturated fat, no. I could see how subscribing to a rigorous but clearly outlined system would have an appeal to someone like Layton. But could science really identify the specific impact of nutrients, molecules, and dosages? Most of the research I came across pointed to the same basic idea: ingesting the right foods might be protective and might help with the side effects of cancer drugs, but there was little empirical evidence that food could cure cancer. Once you've got the disease, no amount of spinach will heal you.

Part of Gerson's appeal is a common fear of drug-based cancer therapies. Chemotherapy is literally toxic, by definition: it is designed to kill off faulty cells. But it destroys healthy cells, too. And one of its side effects is cancer. In this world of ambiguities, Layton pointed out, Gerson was at least a "natural" regime. It would give him something to do besides wait for scans and stew in dread between chemo appointments; it would offer a modicum of imagined control.

And so when the cancer came back and Dr. Davis recommended the vemurafenib, Layton didn't jump on it. He instead went home and read and reread the stories Candace had forwarded him from cancer patients who had tried the therapy and gone into remission. The juicing evangelists had him convinced: this wasn't the option that might work for a few months and then quit on him—this was a potential cure.

At his next appointment with Dr. Davis, Layton brought up this tentative plan. When previous patients had come to Dr. Davis telling her they wanted to do Gerson Therapy, she'd frozen up inside, knowing in her gut that this was an unwise path. In her gentle way, she told Layton she was familiar with the therapy but that she'd read studies that had come back inconclusive on its effectiveness, a response that fed into the skepticism Layton already had. Most of what he'd read, the rave reviews, were anecdotal, he had to admit.

Layton was uncomfortable with the dogmatic adherence people had to any kind of therapy—traditional or alternative. He was familiar with how skeptical Western doctors were of alternative therapy, but he wasn't prepared for the kind of suspicion the alternative therapy crowd cast on Western medicine, too—that its practitioners were evil and in the back pockets of pharmaceutical companies. He just wanted some kind of middle ground. He found that, somewhat, with Dr. Davis. She wasn't happy with Layton being on the Interferon and agreed that, given the stage of cancer he was at, it wasn't clear if vemurafenib would do him much good—certainly not enough to make the side effects worthwhile. She didn't necessarily give him her blessing to try Gerson, but she told him he had to make the right choice for himself.

Earlier in her career, Dr. Davis had tried to talk patients out of alternative therapies, but she felt differently now. "I can't predict your future and know what's best for you in your head," she told him. She had seen Western physicians get cancer and try to treat it by going to alternative therapy clinics in Mexico and taking high-dose vitamin C and mistletoe. She didn't think she would do it, but she also admitted no one could know what they'd do until they were sitting in that seat.

Willie was also concerned at first when Layton and Candace mentioned Gerson Therapy. Was this really what they wanted to do? She longed to go into classic Willie mode, channelling her take-charge former principal self, and call up Dr. Davis directly. "Surely, you've got a drug that works—something that can save him?" she wanted to ask.

But given what few options Layton had, she came around to supporting the decision to try this therapy. Candace reassured Willie she'd researched it and had confidence this was the best choice for the family, which was due to have a new member in mere weeks. She was too far along in her pregnancy to accompany Layton to Mexico before the baby was born, and would be too overwhelmed with raising a newborn afterwards, so she asked if Willie would go. It would be the first trip Layton would ever be taking with his mother, just the two of them.

In July, the month before Layton and Willie were to fly to Mexico and spend time at the Gerson clinic, Layton began a modified form of the treatment at home, following instructions from some of the books Candace had read. The night before this radical lifestyle change would begin, he and Candace went to his parents' house for dinner. His last indulgent meal was not unlike what nineteen-year-old Layton had routinely eaten: pizza and beer. After three slices and two bottles, the last he'd have for some time, he was in a cheeky mood and challenged his father to a foot race down the street. To give Phil, who was many decades his senior, a fair shot at winning, Layton offered to run barefoot in the jeans and T-shirt he'd shown up in. Phil, meanwhile, put on his running shorts and a T-shirt and laced up his sneakers. As they stood at the imaginary start line, between the rows of parked cars, Layton turned towards his dad. "Don't be cheating on me," he said, grinning. And then they tore down the street, the sun low in the mid-summer sky.

"Phil! C'mon!" Willie cheered, clapping.

As the pair raced towards the little crowd awaiting them at the makeshift finish line, Candace could see their matching expressions of steely determination.

"They're too competitive," she said, shaking her head at the strong heredity on display.

Layton won and immediately looked sheepish as he jogged to a stop. Despite always being an ambitious contender, he wasn't the type to gloat or talk smack. He was just happy to run alongside his father.

three

On August 8, 2013, after putting his mother through twenty-three hours of labour, Layton and Candace's baby finally arrived, though he needed help from a vacuum for his grand entrance. As Layton laid eyes on Finn, a swollen, wrinkly mass with copper-coloured hair, his face crumpled. He could feel his own body putting its pain on pause as he scanned the body of this new being: bags like crimped dough under his sleepy eyes. The bottoms of his feet etched with lines so tiny and sharp they looked like they'd been carved into clay by a ceramicist. Slender fingers capped with fingernails that somehow already needed to be trimmed. As family and friends filtered into the room to meet the new baby, Layton couldn't break eye contact with his son, unable to understand how it was possible that he had helped create this being who might one day grow up to look like him, sound like him. When Layton held him to his body, Finn instinctively snuggled into the slightly concave well of Layton's chest, as though he had been programmed to before birth. Layton felt two overwhelming desires at once: to keep his son so small he occupied the same footprint on his chest forever, but also to know, immediately, everything about Finn's life from now until he was an old man.

The family of three spent the night at the hospital together but by the next evening, the potent natural high had faded and Layton's symptoms returned. As much as it pained him to be separated from his son, he could feel what he'd eaten over the last day swirling in his stomach and threatening to creep up his throat. He headed home, where he vomited in the backyard and slept for twelve hours straight. Soon, he reminded himself, his son would be back there with him.

.

Layton spent twenty blissful and harried and sleep-deprived days with Finn before he had to leave him again. With Irma back at the house helping out Candace, Layton and his mother flew to Mexico, to the Health Institute de Tijuana, Mexico, to get training on how to properly administer the therapy he was counting on to save his life.

Layton used an insurance payout to cover the $11,400 bill for Willie and him to make the two-week trip. Aside from their house, it was the family's single biggest expenditure to date, one that Candace had to sell her husband on. The majority of the couple's fights since Layton's diagnosis had been about money. He'd never wanted to be in any kind of debt and spent as little as he could, avoiding anything he thought to be an unnecessary luxury. Candace, meanwhile, still had student loans to pay off. What was another penny in the pot?

Both Willie and Layton were nervous for the trip—not just for what this meant for Layton's health but for what it would be like to spend so much time together in such close quarters. When Layton was in his last year of high school, Willie got a call from his school guidance counsellor one day, asking about a note Willie had apparently signed giving Layton permission to drop an accounting class. Willie went to the school, retrieved the note, and taped it to the microwave for Layton to find when he came home.

"So, who wrote that?" she asked.

"Some girl in the cafeteria," he replied sheepishly.

"You're without a car for the next week."

That was how much of his teenage years had been. Willie took to writing him letters and leaving them at the bottom of the stairs. "Layton, I love you, but you're acting like an arsehole," they'd say, and she'd list the ways in which she felt her son was acting like an arsehole. Later, she'd find a reply left for her in writing: "Dear mom. No, you're acting like the asshole" and an enumeration of the same. When a family friend left her marriage and came to live with the Reids, Layton would often check up on her, make her tea, and Willie would quietly seethe. Her son was capable of kindness, it seemed; he just didn't direct it at her.

Since adolescence, Layton had continued to distance himself from his parents—both psychologically and geographically.

Now, after disappearing for six years, Layton reluctantly renewed his relationship with them. He needed them to take care of him again.

In Tijuana, he and Willie formed an unexpected bond. The clinic's grounds were well-landscaped, with tree canopies carefully pruned into smooth orbs and lush palms and potted succulents scattered in and out of buildings. The buildings themselves felt like accommodations at a two-star resort, which was fine for Layton, who always sought out hostels and budget hotels on his travels. However, the pair were immediately repulsed by the overt religious undertones at the clinic. They didn't come from the Gerson Institute directly, but it seemed a lot of evangelical Christians had been attracted to the therapy. It took away some of the method's legitimacy for Layton—was it just kooks who were into this? Had he just wasted a pile of money coming out here?

Layton was surprised to see people there whose cancers were only at Stage I or II. Gerson, to him, seemed like so dramatic a commitment that it would only be necessary when the stakes were at their highest. He didn't actually want to meet anyone with melanoma—he worried he might compare his situation to theirs. He didn't want to be around anyone who might plant seeds of doubt or negativity, either. Even if he did find people with whom he shared common ground, what was the point of making friends who might then die? And so he became known as "hoodie boy": the loner. Layton was so thankful to have his sarcastic, atheist mother with him. He wasn't technically being antisocial if he was hanging out with her, right? When other participants would gather at sunset on the beach to pray or speak in tongues, Layton and Willie would go for walks along the water to escape them. When in the privacy of their room, they'd mock the evangelical Christians in videos they made daily for their own enjoyment. "Thank you, Jesus!" Willie would say to Layton in her best wide-eyed Bible belt squawk, and he'd dissolve into giggles. Layton got over the lack of privacy in the room he shared with his mother after a few days, instructing her to turn around and face the wall when he was giving himself an enema. Every day, Candace and Irma emailed Layton photos of the newborn, and video chatted with him so he could coo at his son. Layton was desperate to keep this link to the outside world, to remind himself that once this was all over he'd fly back to Halifax and his own version of normalcy.

While it bothered him that everyone at the clinic was so eager to blindly follow whatever the institute prescribed, he thought about other cancer patients back home—didn't they follow what their oncologists told them? Didn't they do chemo or radiation without considering other options because these were the courses of treatment they were expected to pursue?

Layton had already forked over an enormous portion of his savings to be there, but he still felt like he was on a mission for the truth. He'd read what the doubters said on the internet about Gerson, and those questions echoed in his brain. Why weren't there statistics available about patients who had tried the therapy? Why wasn't the research the Gerson Institute did in any of the big-deal health publications? Why hadn't they addressed the academic literature that called the therapy's claims into question? At the start, he was the disruptor, pressing Pedro Cervantes, the Gerson doctor who had been assigned to him, with these questions. When Dr. Cervantes finally gave in a little and told Layton the therapy wasn't going to work for every single person, Layton was taken aback. He didn't want to know that. He was already committed. And that's when he went through a paradigm shift. He had to convince himself unequivocally that this would work. There was no other choice. Though the medical literature suggested he might live only a few months with Stage IV cancer, the team at the Gerson Institute reminded him he needed to follow the strict lifestyle they were prescribing for two years. Layton couldn't help but feel buoyed by the promise of at least two years. He assumed at least some of the friends he told about his decision to pursue Gerson thought it was a bad idea, though none said so outwardly. That's why it was so important for everyone at home to be united in their commitment. He preferred to use the phrase "when this works" rather than "if this works," and he often coached Candace that there could be no outcome besides the one where he was okay.

On Layton and Willie's return journey from Mexico to Halifax, a border agent at the Toronto airport took them aside to go through their bags, which contained several bottles of supplements they were bringing back from the Gerson clinic: niacin, selenium, lugol, and a thyroid supplement, among others. He questioned them about the stash and what it was for, and Willie, flustered, started to get weepy.

"Oh please, ma'am, don't bring on the tears," the agent said, which incensed Willie. Sensing an impending outburst from his mother, Layton pointedly whispered, "Mum, just scale it back. Scale it back. You're going to make it worse."

They were cleared to go through and made it to Halifax with their supplements in tow. After greeting Phil, who had come to fetch them from the airport, Layton turned to Willie. "Mum, I really love you, but I'm never getting on a plane with you again," he said.

Still, both felt their relationship had transformed after the two weeks together. Things were easier now. Layton resisted the urge to ream his mother out when he found her to be over-bearing, and Willie learned to give her son space. She figured out the right moments to give him a hug—the moments when he would let her.

•

When I visited Layton's home for the first time a few months after that, in December, he was dressed as he always was at this time of year—like a mountaineer who had just settled into his tent for the night. His uniform during Halifax's long, wet winters was four layers of shirts (the top one a grey hoodie), long johns under his jeans, a scruffy hat knit in the same style as a braided rag rug, and a pair of comically thick insulated slippers that looked like mini sleeping bags. In this house that was heated only by a wood stove, he was forever cold.

Layton scanned the pile of wet wood stored against the living room wall, looking for any dry options. He was try-ing, in vain, to turn a few pathetic embers into a roaring fire. His efforts were interrupted by the drawn-out wails of Finn, who was now four months old, which carried from the second floor into the living room. The baby was up from his nap. A little while later, Candace came down the stairs with Finn straddling her hip. In photos, his hair was redder and his eyes were brighter, but he was still as sweet and elvish as I'd expected. As he spotted him, Layton smiled so hard it seemed to consume his whole body. He snatched his son from Candace, propped him up in the corner of the grey sofa, and held a soft Cookie Monster toy with large lopsided eyes over the boy's cherubic face. He shook it from side to side, captivated by the way Finn cycled through expressions, as if he were showing off his emotional range to the casting director for a Pampers commercial. Layton knew that in the minutes between hearing Finn's cries and now, Candace had done the hard work of parenting: soothing Finn when he awoke from his nap, changing his puffy diaper, feeding him until he was in a happy breastmilk stupor. But this—producing a smile from this being who was his own DNA reflected back at him—my God, did anything else make him feel more like a father, more alive, than this?

Willie arrived a few minutes later, at 9 a.m., and Gracie bounded over to the door, her back arched, eager for affection. Willie removed her shoes, slipping her socked feet into a pair of Crocs sandals, and walked into the living room to greet us. After peppering me with an enthusiastic "Hello! How are you? How was your flight? Can you believe this snow?" she retreated to the kitchen, her sleeves loosely cuffed a few inches above her wrists, ready to prepare Layton's first juice of the day.

She surveyed the kitchen counter: A few dirty dishes scattered around the sink. A mug, half-filled with cold tea. She blew some of her wiry grey hair, which was cut into a pyramid-shaped bob that stopped at the nape of her neck, out of her eyes. She decided to tackle the dishes later, because Layton's juice had to be served on the hour, lest she set a whole day's carefully calibrated schedule of juices, meals, and supplements out of whack.

Willie had been at this daily schedule of preparing most of Layton's juices and meals for months. A few weeks earlier, Layton had suggested she scale back her duties and he and Candace could take on more themselves; he could tell his mother's arthritis was acting up, her back sore from standing in the kitchen for hours on end. She was insulted by the suggestion. "I'm not ready to do that quite yet," she said.

She opened the door of one of two fridges, which was wallpapered with motivational messages from Candace, scrawled in ballpoint pen on Post-its.

A smooth sea never made a skillful sailor

We will get through this!

The food you eat is the safest and most powerful form of medicine!

The fridges held all the produce Layton required each week for his diet, which was made up mostly of juices and soup: forty-nine pounds of carrots, sixty-three Granny Smith apples, and armloads of leafy greens.

Every surface of the house was covered in small flecks of pungent organic matter: a bit of carrot pulp clinging to a photo frame in the bathroom, pulverized greens crusted onto the duvet cover in the master bedroom, oxidized apple mush on the fridge door. It was spat out by the $3,378 mass of stainless steel that sat on the kitchen counter, the Norwalk Juicer—the Cadillac of juicers. Like a deranged cuckoo clock, the juicer churned on every hour during the day with the house-shaking spews and sputters of a tabletop wood chipper. Anyone who spent more than a few hours here would eventually find bits of fruit and vegetable gunk on their clothes, hair, and face.

It turns out gruel is a real food—not just one from Dickensian fiction. It was listed on the detailed two-page timetable Willie taped just above the range in Layton's kitchen (the gruel, essentially the strained by-product of oatmeal, could be taken as an afternoon or evening snack). The guide was marked with custom pen notations: at 3 p.m. and 4 p.m., when Layton popped liver capsules, he should skip adding potassium drops to his carrot juice, for example, since his potassium levels were elevated. He couldn't have cucumbers because they were deemed to be too high in sodium.

Layton preferred his potatoes whipped because he could pack away a lot to fill himself up—eating involved such calculations now. There was always a large amount of liquid sloshing around in his belly from the juices, which made him feel constantly bloated but seldom full. Even when his mom made whipped potatoes, it could still take him an hour to eat a meal because all the food he consumed was so bland. In the early days, the meals were what Layton imagined might be served at a North Korean prison camp, but either his palate adjusted or Willie got better at finding ways to make the rigidly regimented food easier to swallow. She'd sometimes add a bit of seasoning to a dish, a flourish that wasn't in the prescribed recipe. Though Layton appreciated the effort, he was scared of any deviation from Gerson's strict measures and wanted to tell his mother to stop, but he feared hurting her feelings.

Soon after he started Gerson, Layton had an appointment with Dr. Davis, where he complained about coughing and vomiting up blood, having difficulty breathing, and feeling pain in many parts of his body. In his first phone consultation with the Gerson Institute, his case managers dismissed all of that as healing reactions. What actually concerned them was that his blood tests showed his protein was too high. The culprit was the four portions of oatmeal he was eating a day for the calories, so he had to cut back.

A part of Layton's brain always lit up when he saw foods he couldn't eat, but the feeling usually passed. If Candace wanted a few squares of fair trade chocolate from the pantry or Willie prepared a meal for Candace that had vegan cheese in it—the kind Layton used to love—they tried to tip-toe around him, like he was a recovering addict who might relapse if exposed to the wrong stimulation. He insisted he got satisfaction from simply smelling things—a salty whiff of well-seasoned potato wedges or the caramelized sweetness of muffins fresh out of the oven.

Before he got sick, when Layton went grocery shopping, his goal was always to bring home the lowest possible bill. He bought only generic store brands—mostly boxes of pasta and quinoa. Candace had trouble digesting dairy, so he'd never buy milk products, and she was a vegetarian, so there was rarely meat in the house. Despite these restrictions, Layton's mind was blown the first time he saw the receipt after Candace went grocery shopping: everything was organic and she'd splurged on obscure brands he'd never heard of from the health food aisles. And so when he was sick and realized how much his wife's spending would sink them, he tried to get her to be more restrained. "You know, our lifestyle is never going to be the same," he told Candace. "If you want to sustain this healthy lifestyle, you're going to have to give up on other things."

The grocery shopping was outsourced to Layton's parents, who visited a mix of health food stores and grocers a few times a week. One December morning, Willie came over and held out a surprise for Candace.

"Organic chives!" Willie said. "Our lives are complete!"

"Yay!" Candace said, clapping, her face lighting up.

Life was punctuated by small joys like this. New organic items at the supermarket. Grapes at a 50 per cent discount. A particularly nice shipment of apples. And Willie tried to insert wit into the drudgery any chance she got. In the summer, when she'd found particularly phallic cucumbers in the garden, she'd save them for Layton in a jar of vinegar. In the winter, she took to calling herself the Juicing Queen and came up with a song to the tune of ABBA's "Dancing Queen." One day during my first visit, after Willie handed Layton one of his afternoon juices, he accepted it with a grin and broke out into song.

"I am the juicing queen, seventeen . . ."

"No, no!" Willie cut him off, faux-exasperated—for my benefit, I think—at his bastardization of the lyrics. "I am the juicing queen, *old but keen*, almost seventy."

A five-pound bag of potatoes would run out after two days. A seven-pound bag of carrots would vanish in one. At the supermarket, Willie negotiated discounts on produce. The cashier would sometimes comment on the twenty-four bags of organic carrots she was buying. "Do you have rabbits?" she'd ask. If Willie was in a good mood, she'd say no and smile. If she was in a wicked mood, she'd say, "My son has advanced cancer and we're doing this diet," with a somber expression. Usually the cashier's eyes would bug out in concern and she'd ask, "What can I give you?"

Saving a few bucks here and there was nice in the moment, but ultimately amounted to nothing in their household. The cost of the food and juices alone came to roughly $430 per week, more than half of which Phil and Willie covered. This was their retirement savings, a portion of which they'd set aside for a trip to Sri Lanka in February to visit a child they sponsored in the country. But Willie couldn't think of any better way to spend the money now, following Layton's diagnosis.

The full-fledged Gerson lifestyle had to be carried out for two years, the institute said, and at that point it could be scaled back. But it demanded extravagant spending on much more than food. Every three months, Layton spent $1,500 on an assortment of supplements. Every purchase, big and small, now needed to be tested against the institute's approval standards. Candace and Layton got rid of their microwave because of the radiation it gave off. They had to switch out all their pots and pans to stainless steel ones, since the institute told them Teflon coating released toxins and carcinogens. When the camping shower—which Layton used to take distilled-water showers—broke, Phil, without a word, went to the store to buy a new one. Because the special Gerson-approved rye bread that Layton ate cost $10 a loaf to ship in from the U.S., Willie learned to make it. Candace wanted to buy a big new rug for the living room, but only the organic, non-toxic ones made the grade and they were outrageously expensive. When sharing a bed became difficult for Layton, who was now having trouble sleeping, Candace brought home an air mattress, but she realized after opening it that it reeked of PVC and so she had to take it back. A memory foam pillow wasn't organic, so it was returned, too. The old juicer wouldn't cut it, which is why they had to buy the Norwalk. To store all the produce Layton's juices required, they bought a second fridge. Every six weeks, they did a phone consultation with Dr. Cervantes, which cost $60.

Candace's earnings were low because she was on maternity leave. Layton had put away only $12,000 before his diagnosis prompted him to quit working. There was an inheritance from his grandmother. He was getting a cheque for $850 each month from the government because he was terminally ill. They'd received $25,000 as a critical illness insurance payout—but they used much of that to pay for the juicer, supplements, coffee, and all the new kitchen appliances they had to purchase. Layton knew their savings would soon run out. But there was nothing he hated more than taking money from others.

Layton and Candace always tried to give Willie envelopes

of cash and she'd refuse them, or finally give in and accept but then stuff the envelope under a clock in their house or sneak it into Candace's purse. A while after Willie's father died, she received some of the inheritance and presented Layton with a cheque. He was overwhelmed and started crying. He sent her an email explaining his reluctance: "i don't know why but getting presents, especially cash has always made me sad. i've spent most of my life getting by on a shoe-string so when money comes my way so easily it just doesn't seem fair, like i haven't done much of anything to deserve it."

After Layton's first cancer diagnosis in 2010, a group of his friends raised money for him, which he also had trouble accepting. But Willie had no patience for her son's resistance to acts of charity now.

"Honey, you've got to suck that up. You've got to get over that," she said, reminding him that now there were three people in the mix—even if he didn't want to take the money, Candace and Finn would eventually need it.

•

When he had a sore throat, Layton was instructed by the Gerson team to gargle with hydrogen peroxide. He had to stop using his beloved pomade (because its ingredients weren't Gerson-approved), which he'd been attached to since he was a teenager: he'd spent hours in front of the mirror, styling his frosted tips before he left the house. Ironically, he could no longer wear sunscreen either because of the chemicals it contained, so he spent most days inside with the curtains drawn.

He was unusually flexible, so these were small sacrifices. Giving up showers was not, though.

Before he went to the Tijuana clinic, Layton had started the part of the therapy he knew would be the worst: switching to once-a-week showers to limit his exposure to fluoridated water. The rest of the time, he used a bowl of water and two hand towels—a miserable, unsanitary system that left his skin soapy and itchy. When it was warm enough, he tried to dunk himself in the lake every few days to at least rinse the soap off since that water was deemed safer than what flowed from the taps at home.

Eventually he got a camping shower, through which he could have showers with distilled water, and was able to clean himself every two or three days, depending on his energy level. He first started boiling water in the kitchen and Willie would help, but some days they'd carelessly forget to close the nozzle and that expensive distilled water Phil picked up in large bottles at a health food store would all spill from the shower onto the floor. Layton would curse under his breath, doing a mental calculation of how much money it cost every time that happened, since the water was $1 for every four litres. He kept a tea kettle in the bedroom for enema water and one day decided to heat water in that for his showers, too— mixing it with cold water to ensure it didn't scald his skin.

Now the system was as streamlined as it would ever be. Layton filled a stainless steel electric kettle with distilled water from the cooler that sat in the corner of the bathroom and plugged it in. When the water began to crackle, still several seconds away from a rolling boil, he unplugged it. Into the top of the camping shower's 11-litre reservoir he poured the warm

water that would eventually be released through a small nozzle connected by a long piece of plastic tubing to the reservoir,
and then hung it on the shower head.

Then he crouched down, his head pointed towards the floor.
The sequence of steps that followed were so joyless that to make
the task a tiny bit more bearable, he imagined he was a butt-
naked Arnold Schwarzenegger at the start of *The Terminator*,
when they beamed him to Earth. He wasn't a pathetic man
crouched vulnerably on the floor of his tub to take the world's
saddest shower; he was the frigging Terminator! He worked a
dollop of shampoo into his dry hair and then opened the nozzle
on the camping shower and let a light stream of warm water
wet his body parts in the same order each time: hands, arms,
chest, pelvis, legs, feet, head—a routine he had gotten down
to just a few seconds. He closed the nozzle, preserving each
millilitre of the water, then stood up, lathered his hair, and
rubbed a bar of Ivory soap over himself, and then returned to
the Arnold position and opened the nozzle again, rinsing off
each body part. At some point, he blocked the nozzle with his
thumb to temporarily stop the water flow and stood, turning so
he could also rinse his lower back and butt crack. No matter
how swift his movements were, how carefully choreographed
this sequence, there were always crevices left uncleaned. Patches
of soapy bubbles unrinsed.

Still, at this point he believed getting conventional therapy
at a cancer clinic would feel strange, whereas the Gerson limita-
tions had come to seem more and more normal and reasonable.
In a way, all these restrictions gave him comfort—they made it
seem like there was a method to the madness.

•

The week before Christmas had been the roughest for Candace since the Gerson journey had begun. She couldn't shake the feeling that this would be the family's last Christmas together. Her parents were coming to visit, and while she'd normally be thrilled to see them, she stressed about how entertaining them would detract from her spending time with Layton—what could be his final months or weeks, even. And then she was thinking ahead to how she and Finn would afford to stay in that house long-term without Layton's income. She wanted to come up with some kind of plan, a schedule, a chart, a to-do list, something to make her feel at ease as she had in the years before Layton got sick. On Christmas Eve, Layton felt so terrible that Candace and Finn left the house to visit her parents at their hotel. But the next day, he rallied. And for four hours, everything was normal. Nobody was focused on Layton. Everyone was eating the same thing.

By this time, Finn was nearly five months old and Layton realized that he and Candace had only had sex once since Finn was born. He wondered if it was the cancer, but Candace believed it had nothing to do with her husband's illness and everything to do with her being a new mom. She was sleep-deprived and stressed, and whenever Finn slept long enough to let her complete one household task, it always seemed like there were thirty more waiting. So much of her life had been upended by the perfect storm of caring for both a newborn and a grown man who was ill.

In the mornings, when preparing Layton's first juice,

Candace walked around with droopy eyelids, while Finn seemed wide awake—like he'd never even entered the first phase of sleep. Throughout the night, when Finn roused for feedings, Candace would nurse him to sleep and then cradle him in one arm as she played Spider Solitaire or Candy Crush on her phone so as not to make any noise that might wake her baby—or Layton. Later, she started wearing headphones so she could watch mindless YouTube videos. She was so tired that when she sat down with Layton to watch *Elf* on his computer, it took them three days to get through it. Making all of Layton's juices was so exhausting for Candace that when Irma visited she would heat up a plate of food for her daughter and feed it to her while she breastfed.

Candace had been the kind of woman who would take the pulp left over from making a green juice and use it to bake home-made vegetable crackers. She used to have a smoothie every morning, but running the blender so early would wake up Layton, who needed his rest. Her friends had organized a meal train for the first four months of Finn's life, dropping off Tupperwares of casseroles and soups at the house. She was grateful but also missed making her own food—exercising the control over her own health in the way she always had.

The gym near their house had a babysitting service, but she was worried Finn would get sick there—and she couldn't leave him alone with Layton. She missed running. She missed quiet. She missed being alone, and being alone with her husband. Candace was eroding.

One day, Willie was in the kitchen with Layton as she prepared a pot of vegetable soup. While she stood over the sink scrubbing potatoes, she recalled how Candace always talked about wanting a big family—mostly because she'd grown up as an only child.

"She's pregnant actually, mom," Layton said, trying to suppress a grin.

"You fucker!" Willie snapped, groaning and rolling her eyes. "I'm sorry. Don't even go there." She caught herself and changed her tone. "I mean, that would be really lovely, but . . ."

Layton nodded, knowing how she would have finished her sentence. *But it's hard enough as it is with just Finn.*

On winter evenings, just before supper, Layton liked to sit in front of the wood stove and fuss over it. He knew it was goofy, but it gave him an old-fashioned sense of being the family patriarch to watch over the fire, to make sure his home was warm. On one such evening when I was in town visiting, Layton stared at the log he'd just placed in, watching the flame lick at it, and explained to me how a good day in the house was one when everyone felt good. Bad days happened when Finn was being particularly fussy or restless, or when Layton would be holed up in his room or lying on the couch feeling miserable.

Candace, who was also in the room but had been sitting silently for a while, spoke up in a small voice. "I feel you kind of set the tone for the day, Layton. Not intentionally, though."

"It used to be you too, with Finn," he said, a defensive tone rising in his voice. "You'd be really frustrated or upset if he wasn't sleeping. I don't necessarily think it's just me."

Candace looked down at her hands. "Well, I mean, if you're

feeling shitty, nobody's going to have a great day. Because no one's happy . . . you know . . ."

Layton was annoyed, it was clear. He didn't like being reminded that so much in the household revolved around him, that his moods were so closely monitored and apparently contagious.

Candace could tell she'd hit a nerve, so she tried to change the subject. Just like Layton had his milestones, she had certain things to look forward to that made getting through the slog of breastfeeding and juicing and diaper-changing more bearable. These days, she liked to fantasize about where the family would go after Layton finished with the rigorous first two years of Gerson, when they could travel to destinations where organic food was readily available and they'd have access to a juicer. Candace raised the subject again.

"Layton, what did we decide? Is it Hawaii or California or both?" she asked.

"For what?" he asked, still moody.

"For our trip, when this is done."

"Is this, like, a fantasy trip?"

"If we have money left," she said, deflating.

"Neither of us are working."

"No, I'll be at work but I can take time off."

"And when is this?"

"When Gerson's done."

"Well I'm still gonna have to be juicing."

"Yeah, I know, but not thirteen times a day," she snapped.

I stared into my lap, for fear that if I looked up, Candace or Layton might try to catch my eye and beckon me to take their side in the argument. This was one of my first days spending time with them and this conversation already felt too intimate to witness.

"What are we going to do?" he asked.

"Hawaii or California. We talked about both."

He didn't want to ruin this for her, but he also couldn't feign excitement. "Yeah, whatever you want," he said, like he was placating a child with an outlandish wish.

Unwilling to let him crush this bit of happiness, Candace went on about how she had read about hotels that have special environmentally friendly bedding. Though she couldn't see him, Layton rolled his eyes.

•

Candace continued to read blogs of Gerson patients, some of whom would casually mention having a hired kitchen helper. She couldn't imagine how people could afford that on top of the groceries. She and Layton certainly couldn't, and so Willie quickly became the nucleus of the family, the reason why they were able to get through the Gerson schedule from week to week. For much of the day, including weekends, she was at the house at work. She started making meals for Candace, too, along the way. Usually by 6 p.m., when she wrapped up, she was teary and her back and shoulders were on fire. But she never put her feet up, even when Layton and Candace could see her posture collapsing, her body begging for a break. When she finally went home in the evening, her mind was still at work. She'd write Layton emails—pep talks of sorts. Finally, after a few months, Layton and Candace successfully convinced her to scale back her duties and she agreed to work until the early afternoon, rather than staying until dinner time.

That first Christmas after starting Gerson, in 2013, Layton gave Willie a handmade card she described to him later as "vintage Layton."

"What's 'vintage Layton?'" he asked with genuine curiosity.

"You show a little bit of what's inside and give love and affection and all that and say, 'Go make my fucking juice,'" she cackled, while he looked down, embarrassed.

But he liked seeing his mother in this mood. He needed to see his mother in this mood. Watching his parents give up so much, Layton would encourage them to take vacations, to pick up the hobbies they'd put on hold for him.

"Stop that," Willie would tell him. "You mustn't feel that way. This is nothing you would not do for your own son."

Layton was always hyper-aware of everyone around him and their emotions. He was always latching on to cues. It helped him navigate weddings, knowing how to position himself to capture intimate moments, but his sixth sense was also helpful at home. He came to recognize a particular type of sniff his mother had—one that to him signalled frustration. Each time he heard it, he thought about how he'd disappeared for six years and returned home to say, "Hey, sorry I was gone for so long. Can you take care of me now?"

Unless everyone was downstairs just laughing and joking and having a great time and fawning over Finn, Layton felt suffocated by guilt that he couldn't help raise his son, that his parents were at his home all day long taking care of him. He knew he was the root of their stress—of everybody's stress—whether or not it was verbalized. His mother had assured him enough times she would do anything for him, but he knew that this full-time job weighed on her. How had he earned this devotion? Why was he even allowed to cash in on his parents' love now? There were days when he didn't even think about having cancer, instead fixated entirely on how terrible he felt depending on others.

But his guilt about his parents was matched by the resentment he felt that his older brother, Matt, wasn't helping out at all. In adulthood, there was little holding the Reid boys, who were two years apart, together.

They'd had a free-range childhood—there were many kids their age on the block and in the summers they'd be outside for much of the day, playing hide-and-seek and tag, wandering into neighbours' backyards, and coming home only for meals.

Trips to Thorburn, the tiny northern Nova Scotia town where Willie's parents lived, were common in the summertime. Unlike in the family's busy west-end Halifax neighbourhood that was overflowing with kids, Matt and Layton were usually the only young people in town, and they relied on each other for entertainment. They'd play war games in the backyard, the woods, the mine where their grandfather had worked as an engineer. When the adults were out for the night and a baby-sitter came over, they'd upend the furniture and hide behind it, throwing imaginary grenades at each other. The boys often bickered in the backseat of the car during the two-hour drive to and from Thorburn, and once, when they hit their parents' last nerve, Phil pulled the car over and Willie ordered the boys to get out. Stunned, they did, and Layton and Matt watched their parents take off without them. After just a hundred metres, Phil stopped the car, of course, so the boys could get back in. They behaved for the rest of the journey.

During the years when Willie worked at a school, she'd borrow a video camera from the A/V department over the summer and the boys would film skits—absurd bits that were inspired by Monty Python but absent any discernible jokes. While Matt was the studious, determined musician in the family, Layton was the kind of kid who dabbled in an activity for a season or two and got bored and moved on to something new. He had a tae kwon do phase. He tried piano, then clarinet and guitar. In elementary school, Layton loved his G.I. Joe figurines, and when playing with them, he'd often toss their high-powered plastic weapons aside and make them engage in hand-to-hand combat, something that got under his big brother's skin. Matt would watch his little brother and try to backseat drive the way he played, all the while building tidy structures with LEGO.

By the time they were both teenagers, their differences became more stark. Matt was the self-conscious wallflower who watched his brother grow into being ultra-confident. He noticed all the little details in the way Layton dressed with a mix of curiosity and vexation, like how he'd wear white flip-flops even when the occasion called for something more formal. Though both were introverts, Layton was the one who more easily made friends, who could show up at a basketball court and start playing pickup with strangers.

Matt, by contrast, was always the serious, by-the-book one and sometimes grew exasperated with his brother's unconventional ways.

As adults, the two didn't see each other very often. When Layton went on his world travels, he'd send Matt the occasional email, but Matt usually came to know what was happening in his baby brother's life through reading his travel blog. After Layton moved back to Halifax, Matt found it difficult to pick up regular conversations with his brother and eventually just leaned on his parents to update him on what Layton was doing. Layton wondered if this was how it was going to be for the rest of their lives. Had the gulf between them become too wide to bridge?

•

A vegetal smell hung in Layton's kitchen, except for that time in the morning when Willie prepared the daily brew. This particular brand of organic therapeutic coffee smelled less like Folgers or Maxwell House and more like that stale odour that clings to your clothes after you've spent an afternoon in a coffee shop. The beans were minimally roasted, and according to the company the average cup contained 48 per cent more caffeine than medium roast organic coffee, though it was not meant to be drunk. Because Gerson required it, Layton consumed 225 millilitres of the hot coffee five times a day through his rectum.

After a few months, he had done enemas so many times it was like his body was on autopilot. He'd lube up with Vaseline, hang the enema bucket from the shower head, stick the probe into his butt, unclamp it, the coffee would flow in, then he'd clench up for twelve to fifteen minutes while lying on his side on the floor. After the time was up, he'd sit on the toilet, waiting for a bowel movement. He got to know the rhythm of his system in a way he never had before. If the temperature of the coffee he'd prepared for an enema was too high, his body would essentially say no when he tried to pipe it in. It was like when, if he had a sip of a too-hot drink, he'd instinctively spit it out. He learned that half an hour was the perfect amount of time for coffee to cool to the right temperature, that his body preferred Vaseline as a lubricant over coconut oil. Sometimes, it felt like a game—like, he knew this was what was meant to detox his body so it felt like a small victory if his deposit was especially large. He couldn't quite remember what it was like to have a normal bowel movement anymore—he fantasized about foregoing treatment for a day for the experience.

Layton was always a private person, the kind who didn't even want to change his clothes with Candace in the room, but now things were different. She'd sometimes come into the bathroom and see him in that twelve- to fifteen-minute window after he'd done an enema, lying on the floor, half-naked, his testicles tucked between his legs.

It bothered Willie so much, the idea of Layton uncomfortable on the frigid floor, doing this unpleasant routine every day. When he stayed at his parents' place, they pulled out all the stops to make things more comfortable.

Once, Layton was over at their house when he had to do an enema and Willie put down a small mattress in the bathroom—but Layton just thought it would make things messier.

In his room he found a blue bucket with a piece of paper affixed to it with two strips of masking tape. "P-Pot (we'll empty) xo" it said. Layton did pee in it but emptied it himself.

Some days when Willie entered Layton's bedroom to deliver his lunch, she'd walk in on him groaning because of the sharp pains in his stomach. Willie would gasp. Through clenched teeth, Layton would say, "Mum, you can't do that. You have to stop doing that." Willie learned quickly she couldn't show any kind of anxiety because it would intensify her son's. In those moments, she knew to purse her lips and take the compost out, or go to the bathroom, or pick up Finn for a cuddle.

Layton stopped telling her about symptoms after a while, knowing it would only make her worry and frantically search online for an answer or a treatment. After struggling time and time again to explain this to her, he sent her a video he found online about empathy and how sometimes he just needed her to listen, not to always try to find a solution to his problems.

By now he'd learned cancer wasn't the part that was hard to deal with—it was everybody else. What would it be like if he was the only one who knew about his diagnosis? He fantasized about this often, but knew how unrealistic it was. He had to let other people take care of him because he wouldn't survive without them. Months after Layton's birthday, a festive banner still hung above his bed: HAPPY FUCKING BIRTHDAY. It was important to mark this day now and especially this time—he'd survived his Jesus year and made it to thirty-four.

What made accepting help so hard for Layton was knowing in the back of his mind that he might not have the chance to repay his family. He'd made it to thirty-four, sure, but what about thirty-five? Forty? Sixty? He wanted to know he'd be around long enough to see his parents grow old and senile and then to take care of them the way they had taken care of him. It wasn't so much that Layton was the type of person to keep a scorecard on relationships, but it felt selfish, unjust in some way, that he was taking so much without a guarantee that, one day, he'd be able to reciprocate.

Against his wishes, Candace started emailing Willie updates about Layton's symptoms on bad days—it was clear she had difficulty carrying the worry on her own. One week, she called Willie weeping because Layton said he was feeling numbness in his hands, a tingling sensation. She was convinced he had a spinal or brain tumour. Willie, against her better judgment, started Googling. The results, this time, soothed her: it could just be an electrolyte imbalance, she told Candace, which would make sense given the cocktail of supplements Layton was taking.

Layton first noticed the numbness when he was cutting his fingernails—there was so little strength in his right hand. He called up Gerson and they gave him the line they always did— this was a healing reaction. Maybe this was a vitamin D deficiency? Summer was over and the sunlight streaming in from outside was limited. Layton started taking a vitamin D supplement, desperate for an overnight fix. While he wanted to skip his next chest X-ray and just wait another three months for the CT scan that was scheduled, Candace—because of her fears the cancer had most certainly spread—pushed him on it. She planned to talk to Dr. Davis privately about it in hopes that she could help convince Layton.

They liked that Dr. Davis didn't try to talk them out of Gerson. When Layton went in for appointments with her, if he said he was feeling well, she'd say, "You should just keep doing what you're doing, then." At this point, Gerson Therapy was slightly scaled back: Layton went from five enemas a day to four and eliminated one of his morning juices. But Dr. Davis was struck by the fact that her patient was still, in many ways, under house arrest. She thought he wasn't living but instead tethering himself to the house. His cancer didn't appear to be spreading, and so the symptoms he had—fatigue, lack of strength, a weakened immune system—seemed to be caused by Gerson rather than the melanoma it was supposedly treating.

This was the problem with being sick. Layton didn't know what was actually happening inside his body; all he knew was whether he felt physically well or not. If he felt good, he was invincible. But if there was a day with chest pain, or he couldn't feel his finger, the same thought would enter his mind: *I guess I'm dying.* Then he'd remind himself of previous bouts of stomach pain or stabbing in his chest—things he'd taken to be certain markers of his impending death—that he'd quickly recovered from. It wasn't a gnarly new tumour on his lung after all.

•

today was a good day. i don't know why. exactly nothing out of the ordinary happened. it actually started pretty shitty. something got caught in my enema this morning like a seed or something and i had to dump it and put together a whole

new one from scratch which is a practice in patience on
the best of days, let alone at 7 in the morning. i shouted
and threw the thing in the tub and got on my way. after that
though, i dunno, the day just felt lighter. i felt a little lighter.
i've had some emotional days the last week or so. today i felt
a little more at peace i guess. no real chest pain, no real
anxiety. still tired sure, but every day i'm tired. there was
definitely a different kind of energy in me today, a good
energy. i didn't even step outside today. after my enema
i came downstairs thinking candace would be stressed
because you had a long night but my juice was all ready
and my oatmeal was on the way, it was amazing. that hasn't
happened in a while. it's not some great miracle, it just felt
really good. we got some posters that mom and i actually
ordered individually without each other knowing, it was
cute. they arrived on the same day too. it's a great print,
a deer, i think you'll really like it. we'll probably return one
of them. it's big and square and i think it'll look great above
the bed. it's really weird to think that material things matter
at this point, but you know there's something to be said for
filling your home with beautiful things, just to look at, to
enjoy. i pull a surprising amount of enjoyment out of just
looking at nice things, it's weird. it's more comforting than
i thought it would be, to someone who might not be around
real long. i didn't really think about that much today either.
well, ok maybe that's a lie. i have an appointment coming up
which will basically tell us if i'm living or dying. that sounds
dramatic but there you have it. the reason today was such
a good day is because i assumed, i FELT that things were ok,

that this is working and i'm gonna get to grow old and watch
you grow older too. your mind is a powerful tool my friend.
a POWERFUL tool. it can bring you up and just as easily
drag you back down. it's a big ass mystery your mind, to me
anyway. you just gotta do your best to fill it with good shit,
the stuff it needs to convince you everything is good. cause
that's all you're really after, after all. people just wanna
be happy. if that means simply clearing your mind of
everything, that's great. it's easy to fill your mind with
stuff, complications, stress. you wanna simplify your mind.
i do. everything is easier simplified. less thinking, that's
where it's at man! ignorance is bliss, sure, i'll take it.
ignorance can definitely work in your favour when you
let it. it did for me today anyway. it allowed me to be happy.
carefree even. i don't know what'll happen tomorrow but
i do know today was a good day. i love you man. too much.
you're on the dryer right now sleeping, your mom is
watching a movie, first time in forever. thanks for giving
her a break. we owe you one. talk soon bud. Xo

·

The house was beginning to feel like a prison for Layton, and
each day of this endless winter he could feel claustrophobia
closing in on him. One day, he felt like getting outside was a
matter of survival. He was the sort of person who preferred
to spend almost all of his time on his own, but in that house
where Gracie was running around, competing for attention
with Finn, who cried many times a day, where the juicer was

always whirring and spewing, where Candace and Willie were chattering, there was little calm to be had. Often when Layton felt stir-crazy and wanted to go for a walk, Candace would tell him he was too weak to venture outside and advise him to rest, and he usually obliged. This time felt different, though. His body wanted him to stay in bed, but his mind was desperate to be outside. Candace picked up on this.

"Just go," she told him. She recognized the look on his face because she'd felt it many times herself.

She needed to take walks as often as possible to think in peace, even when the sidewalks still hadn't been cleared by city crews. On one day when I was visiting after Christmas, she trekked through the snow-covered park with Gracie and Finn, who was attached to her chest in a baby carrier. He was facing outwards, but Candace could hear him fussing so she bent forward to see his face and noticed his hat had fallen over his eyes and he couldn't see. As soon as she adjusted it, his screaming subsided. At least with this little man, the fixes were easy.

Later, while strapping him into his car seat, Candace noticed his hat had swivelled to the side again, obstructing his vision.

"Poor nugget, neglectful mother strikes again," she cooed before readjusting the hat.

Of course, Layton saw her as anything but neglectful. He had taken to calling her Single Mom or Mother of the Year, while referring to himself as Deadbeat Dad. Candace laughed at the nicknames and sometimes was in on the jokes with Layton, but other times they felt uncomfortably on the nose.

When her son screamed at night, Candace found it impossible to leave him alone. It was always anxiety-provoking for

Layton to hear Finn wailing since he was too ill to help. "Oh, the baby's crying," he'd say, pointing out the obvious, or, "I think he needs to feed now." As this continued long after Finn's newborn days, Willie's heart would break for Candace. She wanted to say, "Honey, you just need to let him cry" but held her tongue.

When Layton confessed to his parents he felt like a failure as a father because he couldn't do much of the physical labour to raise his son, Willie reminded him, "That baby gets to be with his daddy all day long."

For the first several months of Finn's life, Candace resisted the advice of countless sleep training books and friends. After one particularly bad night when Finn's diminutive lungs improbably powered his scream-crying for two hours straight, she abandoned sleep training entirely. After enough failed attempts at putting him to bed in his own crib, Candace took to sleeping with him on the sofa downstairs, leaving Layton the master bedroom for himself.

Sometimes, Candace would tell Layton she was taking the baby out on the road to calm him down. The tiny confines of the black Volkswagen Jetta became her sanctuary, and she'd often take a short drive and then pull over to cry, her sobs competing with Finn's.

Her mother was her lifeline. And she'd use those aimless drives to call her, too, to vent about how tired she was, to confess she was afraid the treatment wasn't working and her husband would soon be dead. Sometimes, Irma would simply listen, knowing her daughter just needed a sympathetic ear. Other times, she'd reassure Candace that if she could hold on for a few more days, she'd be able to take a bit of time off work to come down to visit and help out.

Finn had grown accustomed to being held and rocked in order to sleep, and when Irma visited she'd happily snatch him away from her daughter and agree to hold him for two hours uninterrupted so Candace could nap or be with Layton or, most often, clean the house in the face of everyone's protestations. If Candace woke up in the middle of the night, Irma would be there for her to talk to. Irma didn't know how her daughter kept it all straight: making sure there were enough clean cloth diapers and wipes in the house, but also tracking her husband's medications and appointments.

Sometimes, when Candace would unload on her mother, Irma would respond with a well-meaning line like, "I feel so bad for you" or "I'm really worried about you." On some days, these words were a salve, but on others, they'd hit a nerve and Candace would snap at her. "Gee mom, how can I make *you* feel better?" Irma learned to be more careful in her phrasing, eventually opting for daily texts asking, "how are you doing?" "you okay?" "how are things?"

Candace seized small moments of escape where she could. She yearned for those early days in Finn's life, when he was easily transportable, when she could drive to her parents' place in Prince Edward Island for a few days. The first time she went, Finn was only three months old. It was blissful: Finn was napping every hour and a half, she never had to postpone feeding him because she had to make a juice, and she could take long walks on the boardwalk every day without feeling tethered to the house. But soon the guilt would hit that Willie and Phil were taking care of Layton on their own and she'd reluctantly head home.

Pessimism would come in waves for Layton's parents. Willie's heart and head would have arguments. On days she thought he was doing well, she'd bake a tray of muffins for Candace. When he wasn't, it would take all her resolve to plaster a smile on her face when she reported for duty at the house. They were scared Gerson wouldn't work not just because of what it would mean for Layton but because they anticipated a chorus of "I told you sos" from all the people they knew had quietly questioned their decision so far.

When Layton's symptoms—fatigue, chest pain, stomach pain—seemed to worsen, Phil's thoughts often jumped forward to what might happen after his son died. *What would Candace do?* he wondered. *Would she remarry? Would she go back to being with her parents? Would Willie and I see Finn again?*

Willie thought instead of the immediate consequences following her son's death: how her mind and body would process it. *Billions of people have died before and those people's families have gotten through it. We'll go to yoga. We'll get drunk. We'll survive.*

•

When Layton watched four-month-old Finn, it was like tuning into a nature documentary. His son wasn't into peekaboo yet—he seemed to be generally confused about the sequence of events—but Layton still liked to try it out with him every afternoon. Maybe Tuesday would be the day it worked. Or Wednesday. He could have no permanent expectations of what his son's behaviour would be like because each day Finn was paying attention to new things, having experiences for the first time, trying to figure out what his body was capable of. In this house where the Gerson treatment made life endlessly mundane and regimented, Finn's mere existence provided ample entertainment.

Layton, who had not spent much time around babies before having one of his own, liked to call his son a "slithery fish"—Finn was sometimes happy and sometimes not and his mood was usually tied to whether or not he was moving. Frustrated squawks and high-pitched whines could often be halted mid-note by simply scooping him up off the floor or bed, but then he'd squirm, eager for freedom. Layton hadn't yet been urinated on or defecated on, but then again, it was rare for him to change Finn's diapers—that was typically Candace's domain. What he was unable to do in terms of routine child-minding he'd make up for by doting on his son in the ways he could, he decided. Layton started designing a font for Finn and registered a domain for him, not even knowing if ".com" would be cool once Finn was old enough to know what to do with a website in his name.

Since Finn's birth, Layton had found himself reliving memories from his youth, but now considering them from his father's perspective. When Layton was growing up in the Reid family home, he and Willie were the two goofy, boisterous ones in the house and Matt and Phil were the quieter, more contemplative ones. Before he retired, Phil was a high school math teacher. He was a man of British reserve, of measured responses, never the type to hug his sons or say "I love you."

In his late teens, Layton lived in his parents' attic, and after a night of heavy drinking with friends, he returned home so sloppily drunk he could barely make it up the stairs to his bedroom. After he did, he promptly vomited into a box full of empties. The next day, he didn't have the time or energy to clean up his mess and left it, intending to take care of it when he got home. But Phil discovered it before then, and carried the box downstairs and individually washed and dried each bottle so he could recycle them. All these years later, Layton didn't know if the act was fuelled by his father's unconditional love for him or his commitment to recycling.

He was always amused in adulthood when he'd go to his parents' home for a visit and, when greeting Phil at the door, see that his father never knew what to do. Sometimes, after a too-long pause he'd chuckle and say "Eh!" awkwardly holding his hand up over his head either in a wave or to offer a high five, Layton was never sure which. Layton wanted to be different with Finn: to be less buttoned-up, to smother the boy with affection.

The first time he could remember Phil showing his love openly was when he ran the Boston Marathon, which Layton had convinced him to do. Phil made a short video before he began the race and said, "My son talked me into doing this, so this is for you."

•

In the first few weeks of the new year, Layton developed what he believed to be strep throat and he rarely left his bedroom.

When one of Candace's friends heard that Layton had been feeling down, she rallied a group of Layton's people to buy him a gift: a large print of a beach in Tulum, Mexico, by Layton's idol, the Los Angeles photographer Max Wanger. It was a print Layton had been lusting after for a while. Only a few in the group knew he had cancer—all had simply been told that he was battling a serious case of strep throat as an explanation for the funk he was in. This triggered a torrent of emails from friends who hadn't connected with Layton in months, some offering that they'd had strep before and recovered after a few weeks.

Whatever it was that Layton was fighting made him feel awful physically, but a bigger concern occupied his mind: the possibility that there were new tumours in his body. Responding to emails about how he was feeling was the last thing he wanted to do. He especially didn't want to reply to the emails from people asking if he still had strep. Even after he did recover, what was he supposed to say? "Yeah, the strep's gone but the cancer's still here"?

Sometimes, photographer friends, the ones who were in the know, would come over to visit. They were unsure of how to address Layton's cancer, so they'd go on about jobs they'd booked, gushing about shoots they were proud of or sharing stories of particularly difficult brides—subjects they assumed he would want to hear about, to which he could relate. It was painful for Layton to listen to, especially since it was now the new year and many couples who had gotten engaged over the holidays were contacting him to see if he was free to shoot their weddings.

It seemed easier to just be closed off from friends, because even some of the ones who knew he had cancer didn't check in. And he grew suspicious of the ones who did. When he received an email that simply asked, "How are you feeling today?" he thought for a long time before he replied. Was this person genuine? Did they want an honest answer? Or were they writing to him out of some sense of obligation— because they wanted to pat themselves on the back, to brag to others they'd done a good deed by checking in with their friend who was so sick?

He hated hearing that people were praying for him, and liked to say he'd rather they spent that energy on shopping. He felt like it put too much pressure on him. If he didn't get better . . . did that mean God wasn't real? He and Candace sometimes talked about how they wished they were religious—it might make what they were going through easier. Like, *Okay, someone's looking out for us. If we don't do well here, at least we'll be taken care of in the afterlife.* But for now, he could do without the pressure to prove the existence of God.

People told him they'd like to help, but he felt it was on a superficial level. They wanted to drop by maybe once a month at the most just to hang out, even though what he really wanted to task them with was coming on a regular basis to relieve his mom of her duties. Some of Willie's friends had offered to do some of the cooking, but it was such an onerous schedule and she was so organized that she didn't even know how she could outsource parts of it.

Layton wondered how easy and joyous outsiders imagined his life to be when observing it only through Facebook. The website could be either a condensed best-of version of one's life or a repository for bitching. He didn't want it to be the latter. And so he posted a beautiful photo of Finn every now and then. *Look at my sweet family! Isn't my son adorable? Don't our lives look playful and carefree and filled with love?* But what people didn't know was that Layton almost depleted his energy stores on some days shooting just four photos of Finn in an hour, and that he used what little verve was left to post one of those photos. He fantasized about writing one bitingly honest Facebook post that would go up on the day he died. He'd have the last word, and he wouldn't have to hear anybody say they were praying for him.

There were a lot of things he wanted to talk about and share on Facebook, but he knew he couldn't because if he wanted to go back to work on the other side of this, he needed to project that he was healthy now. Layton had been certain he'd return to work by the summer, when he'd be able to shoot weddings for the clients who had been sending him inquiries through his site. They, like the ones he'd lined up before, were the ideal types: those getting married on the beach, in backyards, at summer camps. Who would want to book the photographer with Stage IV melanoma to shoot their wedding a year in advance?

•

By mid-February, all the emotional pumping up Layton had done for himself was starting to deflate. The doctor had taken a swab and confirmed Layton didn't have strep throat. Just a cold that had run rampant in his body, which was so very weak now.

Layton got better, but then a few weeks later he caught another bug. Colds didn't feel like they did when he was young and healthy; now there was always the possibility something more was going wrong inside him, something he might never recover from. He had little faith in his immune system. If it couldn't protect him from a stupid cold virus, how the hell was it doing in this fight against cancer? It had been six weeks since he'd done his last set of scans—a CT and MRI of his head, spine, and back—and he was growing impatient that the results hadn't yet been provided. He was at the point now that he was certain his body was flooded with tumours. He'd lost all hope.

It was unexpected that they scanned his brain, which now planted the same fear in him that Candace had: maybe the numbness in his finger was tied to tumours in his spine. He was hypersensitive to what was happening in his body. He'd developed a rash on his chest, just above the lung where he knew there was a tumour. When his back was sore, he'd think, *Oh, there must be a new tumour there.* His mind, which he had relied on to stay positive, to deny death as a possibility, was now playing tricks on him.

Layton started to forget what his son's milky skin felt like. He didn't want his weakened immune system to have to fight any side battles, and spending time with Finn, who had a slight sniffle, would mean sending his war-weary white blood cells to the front lines. So he was in exile.

Before he got sick, Layton used to light up as if he hadn't seen his son in weeks each time Candace carried him into the room. "Oh, hi sweetie!" he'd say in a goofy cartoon voice, kissing his son's tiny smooth fingers. He'd sworn he would never talk in a baby voice and warned Candace she'd better not either, but here they both were, unable to speak to their son in adult tones. Phil melted watching these interactions with Finn—he couldn't recall ever seeing Layton kiss Candace, even. It never got old to see Layton's face transform when he saw Finn, an expression of awe spreading across it, like, "Did I really make this human?"

Now, it was agonizing for Layton to hear the sounds of Finn gurgling and fussing on the other side of his bedroom door, the creaks in the wooden floor late at night as Candace sleepily shuffled around with the baby on her hip. Though they were all under the same roof, Layton barely saw Candace and Finn anymore—it might be only twice a day—and when they were together, Candace and Layton wore masks. To cheer him up, Candace would give Layton the video baby monitor, which he called the Finniecam, so he could still watch his son—in a strange, ghost-hunter-style image—even when he couldn't physically be with him. When he heard his son wailing and weary Candace trying to calm him, he felt all the more helpless. Sequestered in his room, he couldn't even give his wife a sympathetic smile.

Gerson told him to treat his symptoms with echinacea, elderberry, and vitamin C, which he did, but he also decided it was time to return to the practice of writing letters to Finn and Candace, just in case something happened to him. The problem was, when he had a bad day, he had no inspiration to write. He worried his tone would come off as too angry or bleak, that he wouldn't be able to express his affection in quite the right way. Some days, it was just a matter of not having the energy to put pen to paper. But the frustrating irony was that when he did feel well, he'd get this sense of hope that he'd be fine, that the letters weren't necessary because he'd live to tell Finn and Candace those things anyway. It became unbearable to be on Facebook. People were posting things about eating vegan or raising their child with religion. It wasn't fun anymore. It wasn't the escape he needed it to be, and so he decided to quit the social network for a month, even though that would make his already tiny world even tinier. Maybe he'd just stay off the internet as a whole.

He dreamed about seeing his friends again when he was in remission. When he was no longer tied to the juicer and could go to a barbecue. He imagined walking into a friend's backyard and everyone standing up and cheering, "Lay-ton! Lay-ton!" The only good part of his day now was in that fleeting moment when his eyes blinked open and his body stirred. As soon as he awoke, he felt blissed out, like the slumber reset any of the previous days' ailments. But then he'd sit up, or turn over and feel some tightness or numbness or discomfort, and the day was shot. He felt so terrible he'd go four days without showering and could feel dirt accumulating in all the crevices of his body. The task of bathing himself was so finicky and unsatisfying that it now seemed pointless.

He was ready to quit Gerson. He decided there were only two ways he'd stay in it: if the scans showed there was no change at all in his body, or if there *were* new tumours but the one on his lung had not changed. That would be an indication the therapy was working in some way, he calculated. But even if Gerson failed, he was nervous about starting some other kind of treatment. He'd only take a drug if it was absolutely necessary, if the odds of it working were strong. He wanted to at least have a little bit of time being alive without feeling terrible—he'd forgotten what it was like. Two days in a row of feeling good was a miracle. Layton from a different time would've wanted to fly to New Zealand or stand on top of a volcano, but this new Layton just wanted to hang out at the house with Candace and Finn, maybe go to the park if they felt like it.

Still, he studied the map on his wall often. His eyes traced a path from the Maritimes to the Caribbean. The next place on his list was Jamaica, where he dreamed of taking street photos in Montego Bay. He'd already looked it up: airfare was pretty cheap from Halifax, and so was accommodation. Of course, this wouldn't be an Old Layton vacation; it would be New Layton, who now also travelled with Candace and Finn. They'd stay at a resort, the type of place he thought he hated until he went to the one with Candace just after they were married. They would have drinks with tiny festive umbrellas in them— drinks that didn't have any pulverized carrot in them.

•

For weeks, Candace and Layton had been privately thinking the worst, but each knew they couldn't talk to the other about it. Candace woke up in the middle of the night, the only time she knew she had some privacy in her own home, and cried, trying to work things out in her head—different scenarios of what would happen if it turned out Layton had only a few months left to live. Those fears were right on cue: whenever they expected the results of a scan, the prospect of Layton's impending death consumed their thoughts. They couldn't talk about the future, even about the summer. Anything beyond today, tomorrow, and this week was understood to be off limits. There were some days when Layton and Candace barely spoke to each other. Not only were the two suffering with worry but they were doing it separately. Willie kept telling the couple that Gerson was working, though her spirited encouragement did little to convince them.

Candace had joined Layton in a resolution they called Facebook-free February—her psyche needed the break too. But her motivations were the opposite of Layton's: all she wanted from the platform was to see puppies doing flips, or her friends' smiling kids. She didn't want to chance upon petitions about animal abuse, or a viral video about a girl's dying wish being granted. The world outside her home should be light and happy.

On a Tuesday morning, snow blanketed their yard and Candace put Finn into his snowsuit to take him outside for a walk. Something about the way he looked bundled up and his delight at seeing the fresh powder helped Candace break out of her sour mood for a little while. It was the first time she'd been laughing and having fun in what felt like weeks. After they came in, Candace went to put Finn down to sleep and noticed a missed call on her phone—she usually had the ringer off because she feared it would rouse Finn from a nap. She didn't recognize the number, and when she checked her voicemail, there was a message from Dr. Davis. The results from

Layton's last CT and MRI had come back. There were no new tumours, she said, and only a slight change in the tumour on Layton's lung. The plates in his back were tweaked, and that was what was likely the culprit when it came to his finger numbness. "This is very positive news," Dr. Davis said, and promised to call back.

Candace hung up and started screaming, her arms up in triumph. "YEAHHHHHH!"

Finn, who had just nodded off, was awakened and started crying. Layton came into the room, tissues stuffed up each of his nostrils (for both practical and goofy reasons), to find his wife jumping up and down, her eyes wide with excitement.

"No new tumours!" she screamed, unbothered in this moment by her wailing baby. "And only a slight change in the lung!"

Layton was in shock. And then he hung on to the second sentence. A slight change? What was the change? Was it bigger? How much bigger?

Candace dismissed him. "You know what? We know things are okay right now. Let's worry about that later. Let's not focus on numbers right now. Let's be happy."

But it was hard. Because first there was relief, but then came the competing knowledge that there were always ups and downs, that he couldn't fully celebrate anything. And then worse, there was this little voice in Layton's head, the one that was responsible for all his fears and doubts and anxieties. In that moment, when Candace was still vibrating with joy, it was asking him, "Do you deserve this?"

•

In March, when they decided it was time to give sleep training another shot, it became unbearable for Layton to be in the same house as Finn when he was on one of his crying jags. He bought the highest-rated earplugs for sleeping, but still Finn's heaving chimpanzee screams broke through, and an hour or two of that a night ruined Layton for the next day. As a last resort, he started sleeping at his parents' house. After his 8 p.m. enema, he'd drive there and then return home at 6:45 the next morning. Everything in life felt lighter now—for six weeks he'd been convinced he was dying, and now there was hope again.

With this good news, Candace and Layton let their guards down and treated each other normally again.

"I can always tell when I'm feeling better because you start nagging," he'd say to Candace.

"I can tell when you're feeling better because you start not being mean to me," she'd say. Instead, his teasing would be gentler—a light-hearted jab about an outfit she was wearing.

But the peace didn't last long. Layton sensed that since his mom had scaled back her assistance—she was only coming by the house for three and a half hours a day now—Candace faced a bigger burden. He could tell she felt really alone and isolated, and he felt he'd become the target for her stress outbursts.

One morning, Layton, tired of taking it, snapped back at her. "Don't fucking dump on me! Sorry but we're not on the same plane, you and me. You need to find an outlet that you can shit on that's not me."

"Who the fuck am I supposed to talk to?" she asked, fuming.

And that's when Layton suggested me. It was a strange spot to be in. He shared so much with me—sometimes, he confessed, more than he did with Candace and his parents—that our friendship had evolved into something I hadn't expected or prepared for. I recorded most of our conversations and took notes every time we talked, whether I was scrawling them in a notebook or typing them in my laptop. I was now emotionally invested in Layton in the way I was with any of my close friends. Though he had seven years on me, I thought of him like a younger brother I adored and felt protective of. Still, I never lost sight of the fact that I was also writing about him and his family. Sometimes, I wondered if *he* routinely forgot that, despite constant reminders that I was planning to document his story. Or maybe there was some kind of logic that governed all of this: these were intimate confessions now, but months or years down the road, after conflicts were resolved and feelings couldn't be hurt, it was okay for me to publish them. He often told me I was the closest thing he had to a shrink, and while I was flattered that he trusted me so much, hearing this also made me squirm.

When Layton spoke to me on video chat, he was careful to drop his voice low when mentioning Candace. He'd sometimes pause, look out the door, and then continue on.

"Candace doesn't resent Mum, but I think she takes her for granted," he said.

The thing was, he liked staying at his parents' house, an arrangement that seemed less disruptive for everyone. The possibility of moving into their place on a more permanent basis was never discussed upon his and Willie's return from Mexico, although Layton thought it would be the best decision for him. He didn't raise it, knowing Candace would never approve.

To Candace, it felt like her family wasn't whole anymore, that Layton didn't live with them. Every few days, she would ask how long he planned to sleep at his parents' place, and every few days, Layton would offer an evasive answer. "We're just going day to day," he'd say, or, "We'll just see how it rolls with Finnie." On these days, she'd think, *We'll get to our relationship when all of this is over.* It was her coping strategy: to think of Layton's sickness, of his being on Gerson, as a temporary impasse.

Living with Layton could be like living with a brooding teen: some days his mood would be great, and the next, inexplicably, he'd hunker down in his room, eat meals by himself, and speak only sparingly to his family. Sometimes he had stomach pains or woke up with throbbing temples, and sometimes he never explained what the problem was at all. It was difficult for Candace not to be bitter when he got this way, not to take her frustration out on him. She'd feel guilty about even having those thoughts, for losing her temper with him when really, none of this was his fault. But at the same time, wasn't she a person too? Wasn't she an equal partner in this marriage? Was it so unreasonable for her to have baseline expectations of what things would be like?

The financial cost of Gerson came up constantly in their fights. How sustainable it was, how long they could reasonably keep it going before they were in serious debt, how much debt was worth getting into. Dr. Cervantes had said that after two years the therapy could be scaled down even further than it already had been, to seven juices and two enemas a day, depending on whether Layton was able and willing to keep that up. It would be less work than what he was doing now, but would still be extremely demanding and expensive. Layton and Candace gave Willie and Phil a fixed monthly payment of about $500 to $800 a month to get Gerson groceries, even though they knew it still wasn't enough. The cost of the juicing alone was about $218 per week. In the first year, Gerson Therapy had cost $45,266. The cost of maintaining the diet after the first two years would be $19,200 annually. At the moment, the $850/month terminal illness benefit would barely cover the cost of having Finn in daycare.

Layton had lost his wedding band not long after he got married, and finally, two years later, he went to Charm Diamond Centre in the mall to find out how much it would cost to replace it. Learning the price would be $300, he left the store empty-handed. Every time Candace brought up some kind of spending that didn't have to do with Gerson—repairs to the house, a new car—Layton would snap. "Slow the fuck down! Let me see if I can make it through the year before you drop this stuff on me."

Once, on a short drive together after he'd started Gerson, they looked out the window and Candace mused about this house and that and which neighbourhoods in the city she liked. They spent a lot of time watching *Income Property* episodes on Layton's computer, and she would always gush over the homes, fantasizing about moving into a bigger, better one someday. But Layton didn't have dreams that ambitious. He said if they could somehow connect their house to the well system, everything would be perfect—he'd be able to take showers without worrying about the water being fluoridated. He shared this with Candace, who wasn't quite as excited.

"Don't you want to do other stuff? Doesn't this frustrate you?" she asked.

"No, I don't want much more than this," he said. The fight escalated, exposing how the two had different views of what should come next in their lives.

Later that day, Candace, tired of quarrelling, handed Layton a note. "Sorry, I don't know what's wrong with me," it said. "I love you and I love our life." For at least a few months, she stopped mentioning her desire for a bigger house, a better life.

•

Candace worried about the emotional changes the cancer—or maybe it was the therapy?—had brought on in Layton. He'd never had a temper before, but it flared up constantly now. It wasn't because of his diagnosis itself, but because of how the diagnosis had made him depend on so many people. Willie had noticed it, too. For a son who had been so mellow, so mild-mannered, the occasional rage outbursts were difficult to get used to.

One morning, Willie arrived and found the "juice condom" as they called it, the bag filled with all the fibres from the juicer, which was always supposed to be washed and dried immediately after use, lying in the freezer in a twisted mess. Candace sidled up to her mother-in-law to whisper that Layton had gotten angry the night before, and was throwing things around the house in his fury. Another time, she and Layton got into a debate about healing reactions. Layton said he doubted they were always a real thing. Willie countered that they were, that this was the body reacting to changes. "And sometimes they can bring out moods, too," she said, giving him a look. He chewed her out and she knew not to bring it up again.

One Saturday night, one of Candace's friends had a bachelorette party, but she decided not to go. She didn't want to leave Finn with Layton because he was tired and was going to sleep at his parents' house. When she hinted at her disappointment after the fact, he got irritated.

"I would've stayed, but you didn't ask!" he said.

"I didn't ask because you didn't offer!" she retorted.

He'd made an effort to encourage Candace to go out with her friends, to have a drink, but she rarely did. She always felt like she had too much responsibility. To make it possible for her to attend the wedding of the friend whose bachelorette she'd missed, her mother came up for the weekend to look after Finn. Candace had hoped to be out until the wee hours, but she returned home at 10 p.m., realizing weddings weren't much fun without a date.

The thing was, Candace was finding it hard to relate to people too. The rare time she joined friends for a night out, she felt awkward: her friends' partners were usually there, and it was lonely going on her own and being reminded every minute that nothing about her relationship or home life was normal.

Even when completing the routine tasks of life, Candace was forced to think about life without Layton. When filling out forms for her pension, for example, she had to assign her next of kin. She longed to have more children but realized it wasn't a good topic to discuss with him. She'd reassure herself that it wouldn't even be possible in the next year so it wasn't worth bringing up.

But bottled feelings eventually lead to a blowout. In May, Finn's newborn clothes were neatly folded in his drawers, even though he'd long outgrown them, and Layton confronted her about why she wasn't getting rid of them.

"I'm not ready to close that door," she confessed.

"No way," he said.

"Well, that's what I want," she said, carried by an unexpected gust of bravery.

She tried to frame the situation to him in a way that left his sickness out of the equation. What would happen when their parents died? she asked. "Finn would be our only family, which is sad."

Layton left the room, shaking his head. He was perplexed. Candace was already in over her head in this first round of motherhood—especially having to take care of him as well. *How could she possibly want a second child?* he wondered. He knew that even if the miracle scenario came through, if his next two CT scans came back clear and he was deemed cancer-free, he still didn't want more children. He'd have a vasectomy or Candace would have her tubes tied.

Layton never expected to have a son, or a mortgage or a dog or a wife. Both cancer and Candace had anchored him, brought him the life he'd tried to run from but that he had grown to love—something he was loath to admit. But things felt complete now. This was all he needed. Why wasn't this enough for her, too?

Candace found little escapes throughout the week to stay sane, to remind herself of the life she had outside of Layton's illness. She'd go grocery shopping and take Finn out for drives or walks with Gracie. Layton, meanwhile, had become a full-out recluse. At the end of the year, he drove to California Cuts for a cheap haircut but came out looking like a cartoon character. He hated his new look, and then, as a joke, he agreed to have his childhood friend Matt, one of the few who regularly checked in on him, shave Finn's name into the back of his head, which made him look like he'd been mauled by a bear. It wasn't like Layton went outside, so he figured the less hair he had to maintain, the better. Most of the time, the look was hidden under his toque, but when it wasn't, it sometimes caught Candace off guard, making her smile.

Now that Layton had decided to avoid the internet altogether, he found strange new ways to entertain himself. One day, he kept a "pee diary"—a small scrap of paper where he made a tally of how many times he urinated (it was twenty-five). Sometimes, he'd bring his iPad into the bathroom at enema time and take selfies, later applying filters to them to make his head look like Frankenstein's monster, or like he was on the cover of an electronica album. After many consecutive days at home, he wondered if he was going crazy. There was a paper lantern hung in the backyard, which Layton could see from his room, and at night, when it was lit, it looked like a ghost to him. At most, he'd go for a stroll to the nearby lake, and sometimes he wouldn't see a single soul on the journey.

These walks could be exhausting, but even as he grew winded on them, he longed to run.

As a kid, he was never great at organized team sports—there was too much pressure, and sometimes his personality clashed with other players on his own team. He was on the school basketball and volleyball teams, but he always preferred playing pickup ball or running. He liked running because it exhausted him and he always, always felt better afterwards. He didn't need anyone else, or even any particular equipment, to do it. Sometimes, he'd go to the local Running Room to go on a group run, less for the social aspect and more because he liked running with people who were faster than him—it pushed him to drop his times. For the same reason, in Montreal, he joined the cross-country team. So many of the people on it were much faster than him, and it was through running with them that he was able to break some of his own records. He could be with other people while still alone. When he was twenty-seven, he ran a marathon in Halifax without training for it, for no reason other than to say he had.

Layton didn't like being in public anymore. Hearing inane conversations in line at the grocery checkout or listening to strangers discuss their vacation plans would irk him now in a way they hadn't before. On some evenings when Layton drove from his house to his parents' for the night, there was a short window of time when he could stop into the Halifax Shopping Centre before the photo store closed, to get pictures of Finn printed. It could be the most unnerving moment of the week: what if he ran into someone he knew? He was afraid that the period of withdrawal from society had stripped him of his filters, diminished his ability to make small talk. He was worried he might snap—that instead of saying, "Hey man, how are you?" he might say, "Where the hell have you been for the last eight months?!"

·

It was June, and Finn was ten months old. He was mobile and quick now—when Candace was selecting what clothes to put on him, he'd crawl over to an open diaper bag and tug out a package of wipes, his chubby hands exploring the smooth packaging. And then it would hit him: the discomfort of a soiled diaper. A gentle whine would quickly build into a crescendo of heavy, rocking wails. Candace would quickly take off his diaper, but before she could put a new one on, Finn would twist his body and start bucking his legs, all while sobbing. She'd wave a stuffed rabbit in his face: "Cheeeega cheega cheega cheega," she'd say and wipe him clean. Then Layton, who finally felt like he had energy after a rough winter and spring, would tag in, grabbing his naked, red-faced son, a diaper, and a new set of clothes and carry him into the master bedroom to change him on the bed. As soon as his bottom was enveloped in a diaper, Finn calmed and beamed, a total reversal of mood. Layton would smile, proud to be useful, to do things a dad should do every day. Before pulling a top or a onesie onto Finn, he'd blow raspberries on his navel, delighted by his son's excited squeals.

Layton's newfound ability to contribute to parenting had brought a lightness, a joy, to the house that had been missing for much of Finn's life. At least for now, it had transformed Candace and Layton's relationship. Gracie tried to steal Finn's socks one day, so Layton and Candace made her wear them, like a punishment from a fairy tale. When something good happened at the house, even something as simple as installing a fresh bag in the juicer, which was not unlike using a brand new razor blade, Candace and Layton liked to shout out "All that and a bag of chips!" or "Sweet tooth!" in celebration. When they were living in Ottawa, they went to a varsity basketball game once and got seats on the bleachers directly in front of five guys who were friends with one of the players. The group had made it their goal to humiliate him at every turn in the game—whether or not he was on the court. It became clear early on his nickname was "Sweet tooth": they'd rip off their shirts periodically to reveal the letters S-W-E-E-T painted on their chests. If their friend drank from his water bottle, talked to another player, did anything at all, his friends would start shouting "Sweet tooth!" again and again. These antics were even more entertaining to Candace and Layton than the game, and when they got home, they would shout the phrase at each other when anything wonderful happened, drawing out the double E and double O to make the words as long as possible. Since the cancer's return, the two of them had felt like they were in some sort of purgatory, not creating any new memories or moments in their relationship that they might fondly recall later when they were on the other side. But they had their shared history to buoy them till then, and so they clung to their silly inside jokes crafted years earlier, and revelled in rereading love notes they'd exchanged during their early days of dating. It helped them prove to each other that the old Candace-and-Layton, the unit, still existed.

One morning, Candace was in Finn's room, changing him out of his sleeper into his outfit for the day. "Any requests for clothing?" she asked Layton. He said no but stood behind her with a too-big grin on his face, waiting for her to open the drawer where Finn's clothes were kept. Candace lifted a striped pair of pants from the tidy pile and then glimpsed a patch of shiny beige fabric underneath. Layton, like a child holding his breath, finally released the laugh he'd been containing for several seconds. Candace shook her head like she'd heard the same joke a million times and didn't want to give Layton the satisfaction of even a smirk. She grabbed the piece of fabric and pulled it up—it was a pair of enormous granny panties made of cheap, shiny polyester. This was the sixth time Layton had pulled this prank, and it was still funny to him. He'd put the panties under her pillow once. She retaliated by stuffing them in one of his slippers. There was the time they were placed in Finn's crib. Before the panties, he'd pulled the same stunt with a severed plastic leg—usually inspiring a yelp from Candace when she found it, rather than a groan.

Sometimes, Willie would climb the stairs to bring Layton an afternoon juice and hear him and Candace roaring with laughter in his room. They sounded like they were in their early twenties again. She wanted to capture that sound bite and replay it again and again: to remember her son and her daughter-in-law so happy, so normal.

.

Finn's teeth were coming in—two small, hard protrusions poking through the middle of his bottom gum—but these days, his dad was thinking about his own pearly whites. Layton's teeth had shifted back to their crooked positions since he'd had his braces removed when he was twelve. One day in June, he visited his dentist's office to get a mould made of his teeth so his orthodontist cousin in New York could make him a retainer at cost for about three hundred dollars. He'd always wanted to protect the investment his parents had made in his teeth, but he could never justify the price tag. Now he'd withdrawn so much from the world that his confidence had fallen. Fixing his teeth, he decided, would give him a psychological boost.

As adult contemporary came through the speakers, Layton lay back on a pastel green dentist's chair and peered out a massive window to see the rundown brown brick apartment building across the street. He remembered that building, though it had been a decade and a half since he'd been there. He'd met an old man that day and remembered all this time later how the skin on his face was peeling. He told Layton he had skin cancer, but clarified that it was "not the dangerous kind." Layton had wondered what "the dangerous kind" was at the time, but hadn't asked. Now he knew.

"So, are you doing well, Layton?" the dentist asked cheerfully when she came in. She hadn't seen him since the cancer returned a year earlier, and he picked up on the subtext of her question.

"Actually, no, I have a tumour on my lung," he said, glancing from the mobile of tiny seagulls that hung overhead up at the dentist's eyes. He felt in that moment he could read her mind: she must have wondered why someone would invest in a retainer for the long-term goal of keeping his teeth straight when, by all measures, his days were numbered.

Layton wanted to leap from his chair, rip off the little bib around his neck, and deliver an impassioned speech, as though he were the sympathetic hero in a stage production. "I am constructing a semi-fictional alternative bubble reality future where everything is going to be just fine with me, thank you very much. And even if it sounds completely irrational and wildly optimistic, you should just buy a free ticket and get on board and stop fucking with my positive vibes juju already," was the spirited monologue he imagined.

But he stayed horizontal in the chair and simply smiled. "I know it sounds crazy," he said.

It was becoming more difficult again to maintain the positivity bubble. It ruined Layton's day in March to learn that an actor from a show he watched had died of melanoma, much like it ruined his day in May when he heard a radio report about how melanoma rates were going up. And this week, in June, he learned his next-door neighbour, who had a brain tumour, was apparently in her "final stretch."

At the end of Layton's appointment, the dentist said she could actually make the retainer in-house and she wouldn't charge him for it. He knew she felt sorry for him and he insisted on paying three times before she finally accepted a hundred dollars—far less than he knew the service should cost.

A few days later, Layton woke up with a start in the middle of the night, wondering about his retainer. He hadn't okayed it with Gerson before getting it. What if it was leaching chemicals into his body? What if it was undoing all his hard work? In the same way, every temptation he felt to eat something indulgent—not that those hit him very often—was quashed by this sense that he'd put so much into Gerson but the slightest thing could derail him. It felt sometimes like his cancer was waiting for him to mess up, to eat that chocolate bar or to drink an inadequate amount of juice. At least if he stuck with this regimen as it was prescribed, he couldn't blame himself if the cancer spread.

While she maintained her reassuring way around Layton, Candace was again pulled into contemplating what would happen after her husband died—which seemed like an inevitability in the next few years. Could she still afford to keep the house? She knew that Willie and Phil or her own parents would offer to help with the mortgage, but it didn't feel right to take money from them for something like that. Aside from affordability, she thought it might feel strange to stay there after Layton was gone—she knew this was the house he wanted to grow old in. She confided this to me during a walk with Finn and Gracie through the oceanside park close to the house one afternoon in June while Layton was at home napping. We sat on some rocks along the shore of the Atlantic, Finn out of his stroller and balanced on Candace's lap. Finn chewed thoughtfully on some flavourless teething crackers as the heavy, briny smell of the ocean carried over with each gust of wind. Before leaving the house, Candace had slathered every inch of Finn's exposed skin and hers with sunscreen. It was wild to think back to her twenties, when she and Layton would cover their bodies with accelerator lotion—the opposite of sunscreen—that would turn their skin caramel after a few hours of lying on a towel at the beach.

If Finn weren't in the picture, Candace believed her mind would go to a dark place after her husband's death. When she was finally allowed to give in to grief, to drop the load she'd been carrying, she imagined she'd run away, pack up a few suitcases and move to New Zealand.

"I kind of think about that stuff, but I don't tell Layton. But I need to be prepared for things," she confessed.

She heard that for the first six months after someone died, their families would try to hold on to everything in their memories, to keep that person alive in some way. But after that period, they wanted change—to move on.

"Being in the house would be like still being with him. Selling this house would be . . ." she trailed off, staring at the dark water, patches of sunlight bouncing off it, trying to find the right word.

"Like closure?" I asked.

"Exactly."

·

In their twenties, Layton and Candace loved shopping together at outlet stores, but such a pastime seemed childish now, plus there was no joy in it when they had so many other important things to spend money on. These days, Candace longed to go hiking and dreamed about packing a picnic and going to Purcell's Pond with Layton, Finn, and Gracie to waste away an afternoon. If they packed a juice to go, they could stray from the house for two hours. Once it was warm enough, they went as often as possible.

These excursions became the highlight of Layton's week: they could go out in the neighbourhood and, to cars passing by on the road, appear as though they were a normal, healthy family, Candace walking Gracie while Layton steered the stroller.

The destination was often the park space around the neighbourhood junior high school, the one they hoped Finn would attend in another dozen years. One afternoon, after Layton hit a bump on the road, he popped a wheelie with the stroller and Finn squealed with delight. Layton grinned. He loved being the fun dad. Halfway through the walk, he traded with Candace—the leash for the stroller—until they reached the school yard, where a group of sweaty high school guys were playing volleyball.

One of them, a beefcake, was shirtless, and immediately Layton started wiggling his eyebrows suggestively at Candace without saying a word.

"Let's hang out by the volleyball courts, pretend I'm nursing Finnie," Candace said, running with it.

"That's my girl!" Layton said.

"Anyone thirsty?" she called out, not loud enough for the young men to hear, but enough to make Layton double over in laughter.

Gracie was released from her leash and too excited with her freedom to even know what to do.

"Watch, this is the height of her pleasure," Layton said, winding up with the ball thrower and releasing it into the lake. Gracie's eyes bulged and she gunned for the water, loudly splashing and running back over.

"Oooh papa, that's a long one!" Candace said admiringly of Layton's throw.

"That's what she said," Layton said, grinning.

On afternoons out like this, Candace liked to fantasize about hosting Finn's first birthday party in the park. But with Layton's juicing schedule, the house was a more natural place for it. And then worry set in. Her annoying, irrepressibly logical side was always waiting to throw a wet towel over everything. What if other kids wandered up to use the bathroom, and what if that interfered with one of Layton's scheduled enemas? The escapes from this life were so fleeting.

One day, while Candace was putting Finn down for his afternoon nap, Layton was headed downstairs to put away plates, cutlery, and a glass from lunch when he slipped on the top step. He hit his lower back, then his upper back, and tumbled down the whole length of the stairwell, slamming into the ground floor wall with the arch of his foot, changing direction, and then landing in a sore heap on the doormat.

Candace, hearing all the commotion but wanting to quickly assess how much worry this merited, called out calmly, "Are you okay?"

Layton tried to catch his breath—he'd had the wind knocked out of him. "I don't know," he called back. Every muscle and joint throbbed as he replayed which parts of his body made contact with the unforgiving floor during his long, cartoonish tumble.

As Candace descended the stairs, she came upon a ghastly scene: Layton's motionless body in a pile by the front door—a glass and a few plates smashed and scattered all over the kitchen floor. Both Finn and Gracie, startled by the noise, were now wailing from two separate rooms.

Layton was able to turn his neck enough to peek over his shoulder as he heard Candace come down the stairs and they exchanged a look. Candace was part exasperated—like, it wasn't enough that he had cancer, here was Layton, still accident-prone. But she could tell from her husband's expression the damage wasn't too severe. The strings that hung from the side of his toque were in his mouth now and he sucked them in and out slowly as he tried to gain control of his breath. They smiled at each other.

Candace gingerly stepped over Layton's body on her way to the fridge like he was Gracie's water bowl, as though nothing had happened. All the scares over the years had permanently changed the way she reacted to crises—nothing good came from hysterics, and she could see that Layton wasn't in any immediate danger.

"Two o'clock. It's time to make your juice," she said. There was a beat and the two started laughing, Layton heaving deeply as he did.

Sometimes, they liked to pretend Layton had been cured, one taking the lead in an improv sketch and the other readily joining in. One winter afternoon, Layton was lying on his side on a ratty towel spread on the bathroom floor, post-enema, when something that looked like half a fetal brain came out of his butt and fell onto the towel. It was about four centimetres long, slick and veiny. It very likely could have been his own excrement, but that's not what came to mind at first.

That's it, he thought. *It's a tumour.* He emailed Candace from his iPad: "Okay, I pooped out my tumour, let's celebrate." As always, she obliged. That evening, the two took a giddy stroll around the block, savouring this moment of rare jubilation: indulging a fantasy that maybe cancer was that easy to beat.

The afternoon Layton took a tumble down the stairs, his parents drove him to the hospital and he spent a few hours in emergency before they told him he had a few bruised ribs—nothing serious. He learned he'd finally returned to his pre–stomach surgery weight of 165 pounds. It had taken him two weeks to lose that weight but twelve months to gain it back. There was a strange comfort that came from being here now, for a freak accident like all the ones that sent him to the hospital when he was a kid. For an evening, Layton was able to pretend to be a regular ER patient, not one who had cancer.

•

On July 14, 2014, the one-year anniversary of his starting Gerson, Layton arrived in the kitchen to find that his mother had decorated the chalkboard wall with a celebratory message in multi-coloured chalk, not unlike what a kindergarten teacher would do to welcome her students to the first day of class.

"Gerson: one year down, twelve months to go" it said, with each of the remaining months written out in a different colour, ready to be triumphantly crossed out once they'd passed. Underneath that was a drawing of a pond surrounded by evergreens and a Canadian flag. Candace bought balloons and gave Layton a crown to wear. She'd done the math: he'd completed 1,620 enemas and drunk 1,640 carrot-apple juices,

1,460 green juices, and 1,095 carrot juices that year. But the celebrations didn't last long.

On that same day, Layton's neighbour, the one with a brain tumour, died. Layton had seen her husband walking down the road aimlessly the previous night with a broken look on his face. The funeral wasn't until Friday, and the body was kept in the house until then so family and friends could come visit and mourn. Layton thought about going. It would have been nice, he thought, to have a quiet chat with his neighbour, who could no longer speak or hear or breathe. Maybe he'd feel calmer about facing this reality himself if he was around a dead person. But of course going would mean having to talk to the living as well, which seemed too overwhelming. It was a relief of sorts when Candace told him she thought it would be a terrible idea for him to attend.

All the books Candace read about cancer were about survivors—never the patients who had bad outcomes. But one day, she found a blog kept by a guy doing Gerson to treat his melanoma. She thought it would end well, but it was the opposite case: he had a long, drawn-out, gruesome and painful death that his wife wrote about. It brought Candace down for days. She couldn't tell Layton about it, of course, but confessed to her mom how mixed up it made her feel. It was the intricacies of his death that were so awful—it was one thing to lose Layton, but until that point she hadn't given much thought to the visceral reality of what it would look like.

Candace's uncle died from cancer, and she remembered that the last time she visited him in the hospital, he was jaundiced— yellow skin, yellow eyes. His face was so gaunt that his eyes popped out in a ghastly manner. He talked cheerfully about planting a garden with his grandkids and everyone humoured him, but they knew he'd be gone in a matter of weeks. She knew he wasn't putting on an act to make everyone else feel at ease, but that he actually believed he'd live into the next summer and beyond. It was easier for the family to play along.

Candace worried about how naive Layton was about death, how he had no idea what it actually looked and felt and smelled like. He didn't know it would likely mean wasting away, in pain, on medication and likely in a hospital. The rare times they'd discuss it, Layton gave her the impression he believed he'd suddenly stop breathing one day. She never corrected him.

It wasn't that he had never thought about death at all, but that the act of death was a mystery. He used to dread shooting family formals—those portraits of various combinations of relatives posing with the bride and groom—until he learned that one bride's mother was dying. Suddenly, those stiff, posed group pictures he assumed none of his clients actually looked at took on greater importance for that bride. He made a habit of paying special attention to the oldest guests in attendance at weddings.

Every time Candace and Layton pulled up in the parking lot of the hospital, Candace had the thought, *Why can't we meet Mimi at a coffee shop?* She hated waiting in silence in the doctor's office, or making small talk with her own husband because it was too strange a place for a real conversation. The floor they met Dr. Davis on was the one where patients received chemo, so even if they were only there for a consultation, they had to see these bald, malnourished zombies shuffling around in a weakened state down the hallways. Almost everyone there seemed twice their age.

It was after these visits that Layton yearned most for the comforting positivity of the Gerson Institute, a voice that would assure him he would be cured. On one of those days, Layton called Dr. Cervantes, his Gerson doctor, in Mexico, in hopes of getting a pep talk. Towards the end of the chat, Dr. Cervantes said he had twenty patients with melanoma. "Of those twenty, eight are doing good and four are doing excellent," he said. Layton started to panic. There were eight other patients. Were some of them on the brink of death? Were all of them on the brink of death? Layton quickly passed the phone to Candace. More than anyone else, he needed the Gerson people to be steadfast in their assurance this therapy would work.

Once, in the midst of a low period when his confidence was shaken, Candace gave Layton a self-help book that was about the power of the mind in helping heal the body. But the key line of messaging in the book was lost on Layton because the author wrote about how her dad was diagnosed with Stage IV melanoma and later revealed he died from it.

Layton confronted Candace after he got to that part. "Did you read this book?" he asked her accusingly.

"Yeah, I read this book," Candace replied.

"No, you didn't read this book because you would've told me the author's dad dies from melanoma!" he barked.

For Layton, looking up survivability stats was like stalking an ex's Facebook page. You knew you shouldn't do it, that nothing good would come of it, that what you could find might cause you untold distress, but there was always that urgent curiosity that was so hard to resist.

One of Willie's friends sent Layton a link to a post from his favourite website, Humans of New York, a collection of street photography paired with provocative quotes from the photo subjects. The post was a photo of an old man with a cord attached to his glasses.

"I have stage 3 melanoma, which puts me at a 48% chance of survival over the next 5 years" the post began, effectively ruining Layton's day. The thoughts that followed: If there was only a 48 per cent shot someone with Stage III would live another five years, what did that mean for someone with Stage IV? Surely they were lower. How much lower? And then he stopped himself, as he always did. He didn't want to know what the odds were.

Denial had become a religion for Layton. In some part of his brain, he had the awareness it was irrational to believe he'd survive, that he'd grow old, but he had to ignore that part. How could he live knowing he was going to die? Denial sometimes felt like a physical destination: a place he could go to that was comfortable, predictable, where there were no surprises. Being there made it easier to get through each day and each week. It became the one thing that gave him any sense of security.

One week, I went out of my way to avoid speaking to Layton, out of fear I might slip up and mention the death of Jessica Ainscough to him. Ms. Ainscough became known as "The Wellness Warrior," an Australian writer who gained an international following through blogging about her decision to treat cancer through Gerson Therapy. She, like Layton, had travelled to Mexico with her mother to do the training. She wrote extensively about the treatment and her belief it was helping her heal, but a few years later published a gutting post about how aggressively the cancer had returned. She detailed how she had experienced ten months of bleeding from her armpit and had become very weak. When she died shortly thereafter, at thirty, media outlets from around the world covered the news, most devoting several paragraphs to raising their eyebrows about Gerson Therapy.

To mention her death to Layton would be to jab a pin into the protective bubble he'd built for himself. It didn't feel like my place to bring that information to him, but I still tried to make him address the subject of death when I could. One day, as we sat in his living room, Layton told me that when he'd learned he had Stage IV melanoma, he'd had the thought to put a box together for Finn—expecting he might not live long enough for any kind of memory of him to be imprinted in his son's brain. He wrote notes to place inside it, and asked his parents to do the same. The tangibility of such a memento was important to him, which was odd because in his line of work everything was digital. He never even bothered selling wedding prints or photobooks to his clients, instead giving them DVDs or links to folders in the cloud where they could find several hundred wedding snapshots.

What was important to him was leaving behind something that others couldn't dispute or misremember. A box of things from him to his son would be the truth, he thought. Or his truth, anyway. And he wanted Finn to know him without someone else's rosy filter applied.

I asked him to clarify—so he wanted to be remembered in a way that captured both the positive and the negative?

He stiffened. "It's difficult to talk like this because now we're speaking a truth. That what's going to happen to me is inevitable. It's hard for me to think with that polarity."

Was this really the first time he was being asked to go there? Didn't death come up when he talked to other friends? I asked.

"It never does. Nobody is willing to. And that's something that's frustrating, too. Because when something this heavy happens, it's like nothing is taboo anymore."

But then he grew to want things to be that way. At the start, when he'd bring up death with Candace, she'd say, "Don't talk like that, don't talk like that." And he soon realized he didn't want to either.

I asked him once what he'd do if Gerson didn't exist. Would he then take the drug Dr. Davis had offered him at the point of the Stage IV diagnosis?

"Of course," he said, as his eyes widened and his brow furrowed. He seemed surprised and insulted by the question.

"It's not off the table. If I'm flooded with tumours, of course I'm going to shoot myself up."

•

When Layton was doubled over in the backyard in the weeks after his stomach surgery, writhing in pain, it was only Candace's meditation coaching that helped him. The duties of resident cheerleader, of relaxer-in-chief, often fell to her.

The only kind of relaxation technique he would submit

to at home was the one Candace led him through, which was inspired by the Savasana at the end of her yoga classes. Layton would lie on the ground, a log.

"Okay, release the tension in your head," she would tell him, gently pressing her fingers on his scalp and then sliding them down. "You're going to release your head muscles and your face and let go of the stress." She'd coach him through deep breathing, telling him to blow out the tension. She'd help him visualize pushing negative energy out of his body, limb by limb, joint by joint. And then help him imagine his body was healing itself from the inside out.

As effective as Layton said this was, Candace still thought he could benefit from some kind of therapy outside the home. But seeking the help of a counsellor or even a massage therapist was unappealing to Layton—no different from buying a dance at a strip club. He said the therapy could never effectively soothe him if he knew the person administering it was getting paid. Even Candace's free massages were often turned down. If she came up behind him and started to give him one, he'd shrug her off, "Okay, stop, get off my shoulders!" Other times, when he was feeling naughtier, he'd say, "Lower . . . lower . . . now in the front . . ." to make her laugh.

When he met with his family doctor to talk about his stress level and how he needed to keep the embers lit on his business as he went through treatment because he had no other career to fall back on, the doctor offered to write him a prescription for anxiety pills. He passed.

In the summer following his diagnosis, he went to see someone for hypnotherapy, hoping it would help stop some of the anxiety attacks that had come on after his diagnosis. He only lasted one session because the therapist started off asking Layton to close his eyes and picture himself on a beach: a scene he now associated with cancer. When he listened to meditation tapes, in which a man with a soothing voice narrated, Layton couldn't focus, distracted by little tells in the guy's routine that suggested his target audience were people with extreme anxiety, or those who were physically debilitated. He would say things about how it was okay if you were only breathing, if no other part of your body could participate. Layton wanted the tape to be tailored to him. He needed the person to believe in *him*, Layton Reid, the individual.

After much cajoling, Candace convinced him to attend a positivity workshop. The instructor told participants to sit across from someone else in the room and tell them a problem. First, the partner was asked to respond negatively—scoffing, rolling their eyes. In the second round, they were asked to respond positively. Others in the room had stories about getting bullied when they were kids, but although his problem was much more serious, Layton had reached a point where he was tired of bullshitting or sugar-coating his situation to spare people the anguish. He told two others his story, and when they started crying, he found himself forced to comfort them. *Fuck this, I'm not playing this game*, he thought.

Later in that workshop, the participants were asked to write down the name of someone they knew who was a hero and to list the attributes that person had. They were then instructed to cross out the person's name and put their own name at the top, to change the pronouns to personal ones. "I am tenacious" was one of the things Layton wrote down that day, and when he returned home, he made it his mantra. When he went out for walks alone in the cold, sometimes so tired he didn't know if he had the strength to make it back to the house, he'd repeat the phrase in his mind, slowly lifting one leaden foot after the other. "I am tenacious. I am tenacious. I am tenacious."

I have this thing about getting my hair cut at salons.

I hate it. I always have. I'm not sure why really, but it's never not an uncomfortable experience for me. I think it's the intimacy of what takes place and the money exchange that follows. There's just something about having a stranger rub shampoo and conditioner into your scalp then towel dry you, and cut your hair while making small talk that's always had me thinking of all the other things they'd rather be doing if I wasn't paying them to do it for me.

Don't even get me started on massages. Or strip clubs for that matter.

I know, I know, you don't have to say it. I'm weird, I get it, but that's not the point. The point is Candace has been cutting my hair with old blunt kitchen scissors for as long as I can remember. It's not her favorite, but she does it anyway, and that's why I'm mad about her.

Today of all days, I didn't even have to ask. She offered. Imagine that.

Volunteer Valentine's Day hair cuts?

That's what it's all about people.

That's true love.

•

Layton had decided to log back on to the internet in July, but it felt like such a noisy place now. He'd planned a few Skype sessions with photographers who had contacted him out of the blue for advice on shooting weddings. It was nice to know that even after this period of hibernation, of not having shot a wedding in a year, his mark on the internet was still there. But he was also wary of strangers. He saw a post on Facebook from a guy who he'd connected with before he went to the Gerson clinic. He had a layover in San Diego before reaching Mexico, and the two had agreed to meet up there. Then the guy stood him up at his hotel and never provided any explanation. But here he was, posting on Layton's wall. If anything, it reinforced Layton's withdrawal from the internet, from social media. Those connections, it turned out, were so inauthentic anyway.

In elementary school, Layton was part of a gang of five who covered the neighbourhood on their BMX bikes. His two closest friends were a pair of twin brothers, Mike and Matt, who lived a few doors down. In junior high, Layton learned his friends' father was dying of cancer. Once, during a backyard sleepover, the boys' father came outside calling for the cat, slurring his words and sounding drunk. Layton and another friend laughed and mimicked him at the time, and then felt shame when they found out the slurring was due to the cancer treatment the man was receiving. Matt slept over at Layton's house a few months later, and Layton learned the next day that Matt and Mike's father had died that same night.

It was something Layton never knew how to talk to the brothers about. He was a boy who didn't have the language yet. He knew he felt something, but how to articulate it? One day, when walking home from playing basketball with his two friends, who were now fatherless, they got into a fight. Matt broke down and accused Layton of being an asshole for making fun of his father when he was dying. Layton, feeling a mix of sadness for his friend and shame, started crying too. The boys hugged. Decades later, after Layton got sick, Matt would often email him not to *ask* to come over but to *tell* Layton he was coming by. He was the one who shaved Finn's name into Layton's head after the bad haircut.

Layton wished he had that sort of relationship with the other Matt in his life: his brother.

It was hard for Layton not to resent how his brother had behaved when he got sick. Matt was a lot like Phil: he had a caring heart but would usually wait for instructions on how to help. The odd time Matt reached out to his brother, Layton suspected it was at their mother's prompting. After Layton's Stage IV diagnosis, he didn't tell his brother directly—his parents did. And Matt sent a one-line email to him, something that gutted Layton. If their roles were reversed, Layton was sure he would have driven to Matt's house, rung the doorbell, and enveloped his brother in an awkward hug. If his brother got sick, he'd show up.

four

Finn took his first shaky but confident steps at home as his parents watched in utter awe. No one was more surprised than Finn himself, though, who didn't seem to understand how his body could suddenly do this new thing. But Layton didn't get to watch in real time as those steps became more graceful and assured, because the next day he was back in the hospital. A year and a half earlier, no surgeon wanted to go near the tumour on Layton's lung, but a recent scan had shown it had grown and the oncology team said that despite the risks, it was important to remove it. Complications came up during the operation and it stretched from the scheduled two hours to five, but it was ultimately a success.

As he lay in recovery, Layton watched videos Candace sent him documenting Finn's new skill. Candace and Irma would sit a few feet away from each other on the floor of his nursery, their legs forward and knees bent to form a sort of protective aisle so Finn could walk from one of them to the other. He would take a few steps forward, still not knowing to land on his heel rather than the ball of his foot, and sway a little before losing his balance and collapsing in a hug in his mother's or grandmother's arms. By the time Layton returned home, Finn was taking six, seven, eight steps at a time with a spotter standing close by.

As her return to work and Finn's transition to daycare loomed, it was difficult for Candace to come to terms with the fact that Finn was no longer a baby, no longer an appendage whose survival was dependent on her. And that, more than anything, made her long for another baby. But Layton had now made it clear that wasn't going to happen. This wasn't something she could wear him down on like she had with so many things before. What bothered her was that Layton couldn't cut her any slack, couldn't bring himself to see her perspective, or even sympathize with what was a natural hormonal, emotional response to this point of transition. Why did he see her motivations as selfish?

Candace brought up the possibility of marriage counselling, but with so much on both their plates, it seemed like an inaccessible luxury—to even find the time to go to an appointment or coordinate a house call with a therapist was out of reach. The solution was what it had been since Layton began Gerson: Candace gave in and told her husband that their marriage was more important than having another child. As soon as she let it go, she could feel things thaw between them.

Finn had now gotten used to life without his dad, who had

been relegated to a sort of supporting character in his world. At Finn's daycare, there was a corner where they posted pictures of the children's parents and siblings, and if a child ever felt particularly homesick or upset, one of the staff would walk him or her up to the wall to stare at their family snapshot. The idea of that was so heartbreaking to Layton: that these children might be traumatized by being separated from their families for only a few hours. What would happen if it wasn't only one day? What if it was forever? Surely a photo on the wall wouldn't cut it.

The sadder thought: would Finn even take comfort from seeing his father's photo on the wall? Now Layton, in recovery from lung surgery, could see Finn for only about an hour a day after Candace brought him home from daycare. Before, when she carried Finn through the door, he'd screech in excitement at seeing his daddy again, but now he was more subdued. Layton couldn't hold him or play with him or do much more than watch him while they were in the same room together. He'd become a stranger to his son.

Still, it was thrilling to see Finn's independent personality developing. He had his own language he spoke now, a highly articulate baby babble, and he'd mimic his parents and dance and give high fives to anyone who asked for one. This was the motivation to get better that outweighed all the rest. Layton believed that Finn needed him to some small degree, but he needed Finn more.

Candace's parents stayed with them at the house over Christmas, and it was a rough, wild time, with Finn teething, people intermittently battling colds, Finn and his cousins variously throwing tantrums while Candace tried to read to them. When Candace decorated the tree, Finn wept as he watched his mother string the lights around it, frustrated he couldn't quite help in the way he wanted to. His Christmas concert at daycare was pure chaos: children in their Gymboree formal attire, wailing off-key and crying as their parents beamed and took photos and videos on their phones.

•

In a house with a loud, obnoxious dog, a wild toddler, and the frequent presence of two extroverted women, Callie the cat was in many ways the member of the household most like Layton. And so when she died in the new year, Layton took it harder than Candace did. He and Callie could be in each other's company, silent, not needy, but a mutually comforting presence. In Ottawa, in those difficult months following Layton's first diagnosis, Callie would sit on his chest: a warm, furry mound lightly breathing as he watched TV or worked on his laptop. She always found a way to lighten the mood. But as new members moved into the household, the attention she received steadily decreased.

Their veterinarian thought Callie had leukemia and had advised they put her down. At the appointment, Layton found it chilling to see a warm body inhaling oxygen and exhaling carbon dioxide suddenly go cold and still.

When Layton returned home, it was as if Finn knew his father had experienced loss: he reached out to him more to play, to snuggle. Even though Layton knew intellectually that his son was too young to understand death or mourning, he took comfort in explaining this extra affection this way. It was a wonder that this child, who so recently had been a clump of cells, was now showing early signs of empathy. Layton's favourite framed photo in the house was the one of Finn on the day he was born: freshly pulled out of Candace, a wrinkled mass, eyes wide and adjusting to the light and, more broadly, to the world outside his mother's body.

•

In April, Layton went in for a CT scan and he was feeling optimistic. If things came back clear, he'd wind down Gerson and return to something of a normal life again. He'd been figuring out how to re-enter the photography scene—a full-day wedding would be too much for him to dive right into, but maybe he could set up some kind of portrait business, an interesting way of capturing all the guests who attended a wedding.

On the day of the appointment, Candace and Layton took a bottle of champagne with them. Layton had previously joked with his parents, "If it's clean, I'm gonna pop it open. If it's not, I'm going to get on the bridge and jump."

The scan was clean. No cancer. Layton and Candace walked out of the office beaming, playfully shoving each other and saying, "You were scared!" "No, YOU were scared!" They strolled down the bridge, the one Layton now didn't have to jump off, popped the cork on the champagne, and both glugged some down. Layton was aware that he'd feel terrible the next day, but wouldn't it be nice to feel terrible from a good, old-fashioned hangover than from cancer for a change?

They headed to Willie and Phil's. Layton raced up the stairs to the den, the same place where he'd told his parents about the stomach and lung tumours two years earlier, and shared the news with them.

"That's great, that's great," Willie said, smiling, and then she and Phil started talking about other things. Layton's face fell.

"Well, fuck, this is the best news!" he said, annoyed that they weren't understanding the significance of what he'd told them.

Willie reminded him gently that he'd always asked that they not get too high on the highs or too low on the lows. Willie knew she couldn't be too happy about this because things could change at any moment.

Layton had asked the surgeon for a digital copy of his CT scan and received a stark greyscale image of his abdomen: his lungs asymmetrical black masses; his stomach a little blob nestled into his liver; his ribs a string of small rounds, like slices of calamari. Everything looked a little skewed and to the wrong scale, but what was important was that there were no tumours—what had been cut out with surgical instruments had stayed out. He thought about blowing up the scan at Kinko's, sticking it in a big frame and mounting it in the bathroom or living room—visitors might take it to be a macabre art piece, but to him it would be a source of inspiration. Maybe seeing that scan would help his parents understand how huge this news was.

But Willie and Phil had been right to hold back from celebrating with their son. A week later, Layton, Candace, and Finn were playing in the yard when the colour suddenly drained from Layton's face. He told Candace he was tired and needed to sit down, and she followed him inside. As he stood in the kitchen, he suddenly looked up to the ceiling, his neck tracing a circular path as though there was a bird or wasp flying overhead. Then his legs buckled under him and his whole towering frame fell to the kitchen floor and he began convulsing.

Candace called 911 and paramedics were dispatched. Then she called Willie and Phil and explained Layton had had what she thought was a grand mal seizure and that she desperately needed them to come look after Finn because she wanted to ride with Layton to the hospital. Willie, convinced Layton might die in the back of the ambulance, jumped in the car and lurched through rush-hour traffic and then channelled all her strength to be calm and collected for Finn. Later, she and Phil joined Candace at the hospital.

"Is it the brain?" Willie asked Candace, knowing the answer.

"Yeah," she said. And they sat in silence.

All the doctors could say after a CT scan of Layton's brain was that they saw "four spots." They weren't going to use the word "tumour" yet, but at this point, everyone understood that that's what these probably were. Tumours. In Layton's brain. What did it matter now that his abdomen was cancer-free? The news changed everything. All Layton's self-delusions about permanently ridding his body of cancer, of returning to a regular life as a wedding photographer, of growing old with Candace and Finn went out the window that day.

Layton and Candace scheduled a phone consultation with Dr. Cervantes, the Gerson doctor. "We're in trouble," Layton said, and explained the results of the CT scan. Dr. Cervantes told him to do the radiation the oncology team in Halifax had recommended. Layton was surprised to receive such advice from the man who'd been the lone medical professional guiding him on the alternative therapy path for two years, but it was also a relief to have the pressure taken off him and Candace to make the decision about quitting Gerson.

In the days that followed, anger came to him in bursts—he was pissed that Gerson had failed him even though he'd held up his end of the bargain. He found his spot under the tree in the backyard and cried hot, angry tears. He felt a foreign rage course through his bloodstream. He'd obediently downed all his supplements, he'd drunk each glass of carrot juice at the exact prescribed time every single damn day, he'd logged countless hours lying on his side on the bathroom floor for his enemas. And here was the cancer, like a game of Whack-A-Mole, cleared from his abdomen but now popping up in his brain.

He was annoyed that his mother and wife had invested so much time and energy in this process and it hadn't worked. It felt like he, Willie, and Candace had all been on the same page—they all had to believe it was working together because the doubts of one person would erode the strength of the others. They weren't naive to the fact that something could happen. But why acknowledge that openly, or dwell on it?

Candace's feelings mirrored Layton's as she processed what it meant that Gerson had failed. In a way, it felt like they'd done everything for nothing, but then she reminded herself about the options that were available at the time of Layton's Stage IV diagnosis. She told herself that had they not done Gerson, he might have died within a few months, the cancer might have spread faster. This had bought them time. To her, Layton was alive because of Gerson. It had been an empowering choice—the only empowering choice.

For both of them, there was also a deep sense of relief. Layton was free now, like shackles that had been tied to his ankles for two years had finally been unlocked. He'd tried. He'd failed. Now he could move on. In many ways, the world felt new again. It was like getting to do a fresh set of firsts but this time with an adult brain, one that could truly appreciate all these small delights. Now, with his camping shower in the trash, he could stand under the shower head and wash the shampoo from his hair—and then lather it all up a second time if he wanted, knowing there would always be enough water to rinse it out again.

He couldn't flip a switch and eat anything he wanted right away, knowing his body had been tuned in such a way to only be able to process the vegan food and juices he'd subsisted on for so many months. But he'd build up to some of his fantasy foods one day. He dreamed of heading downtown and ordering a chocolate milkshake in a tall glass served alongside the steel cup it was mixed in, which would be filled with surplus shake. Or of making a pilgrimage to a place in the city that had won the local alt-weekly's "best of Halifax" for its burgers. It might be nice to have a beer again.

Candace loved watching Layton eat: a breakfast sandwich, a slice of pizza, a poached egg. For the most part his diet was still organic and sugar-free, but he allowed himself the occasional indulgence, like an ice cream sandwich. He described the first one he bit into to me as "sex in your mouth." "It just jolts you. It's like ding, ding ding ding ding ding! Every cylinder in your brain is firing."

Layton continued doing one daily enema since his digestive system didn't seem to know how to process what he ate without it. The one he kept in his schedule guaranteed a quiet stretch of alone time in the bathroom, the single moment of clarity he got to experience each day.

Two weeks after his seizure, Layton started radiation. It was strange going back to the hospital regularly now, where he got nods and smiles from nurses who recognized him from years earlier. The plan was to target the two smaller tumours (there were four in all; two small and two large), and if the smaller ones shrank or at least stalled in growth, his medical team might take a more targeted approach.

He was tired and extremely weak now, too, like he was during the worst stretches of Gerson. The hushed voice he once reserved for Finn's nap time was the tone he always spoke in. It was as if every sentence drained some of his energy and that when the tank was empty, he would drop dead. He looked like he'd already lost a physical battle: he had red marks on his face, like bear scratches, from the mask he wore for radiation.

His brief honeymoon with foods he'd missed was now over. Layton was so nauseated from the steroids he'd been taking since he started radiation, to reduce brain swelling, that he didn't have much of an appetite. He often left his toast with honey untouched at breakfast, and would pick at a bowl of pasta and vegetables at lunch. Every day, he faced a choice: take medication that would alleviate the nausea but knock him out, or be awake but queasy. If these were his last weeks on Earth, did he want to spend them sleeping? On one visit I made in May, he chose the nauseated option and as our conversation wore on, it was clear that being awake—being alive—was becoming less and less bearable for Layton. As we spoke, his voice grew thinner and his position shifted, his body getting more horizontal on his bed until finally he knew he had to give in and take rest.

I spent time downstairs as he napped, and I worried I'd not have the proper chance to say goodbye to him before I had to leave, but then he roused himself half an hour before my departure and we sat outside, me in a hammock, he in an Adirondack chair pulled up beside it.

When my ride pulled up, we both stared at the ground, shuffling our feet, joking about how awkward this moment was, not knowing how to say "Goodbye . . . maybe forever?" to each other. He looked up at me in a way he never had before, like he was about to cry, and pulled the hood on his sweatshirt over his head, yanking the edges of it down to cloak his eyes, like a little kid might. I hugged him gently, since his body was so fragile now—and then we pulled apart, both trying to find words and failing. Then he playfully shoved me, like a playground bully, muttered, "Get out of here," flashed me a smile, and walked away.

•

In the weeks that followed his seizure and the start of treatment, Layton turned his mind to practical things, like transferring bills from his name to Candace's. A big priority in this new stage was replacing the fixtures in the bathroom, an item that had been on the to-do list for years but that now seemed more pressing than ever. Layton had done more than a thousand enemas in that small space, and it was time to gut it and start with something fresh to mark that period being behind them. One Saturday, a delivery man pulled up to the house and unloaded a new toilet and bathtub on the driveway. From the window, Layton feebly watched, tears streaming down his cheeks, as tiny Candace hauled the two hulking boxes into the house on her own. In a way, it was like he was already gone: a ghost watching his widow.

In May, less than a month after Layton's seizure, Candace was doing laundry—a pile of Finn's tiny socks, his baby jeans, her pyjamas—and all that was in the mix from Layton were his thick grey wool socks. He'd started paring down his possessions—throwing out the rattiest clothes he owned, donating others, saving a few of his favourites for Finn or for friends, like the big purple sweatshirt that had EVERY DAY I'M HUSTLIN' written across it in bold yellow text.

He thought about writing his own obituary, but it was always difficult to find the right mood for such a task. When he was in a garbage mood, he had no motivation or inspiration to write anything. It was when he felt well that he could process his thoughts on paper, even if they were negative, but he struggled to actually write something as heavy as "I'm dead now." He was in the process of getting ready to face the end, but he wasn't there quite yet.

•

Layton began his second round of radiation at the end of June—but it was only one day of treatment. The idea was that if he didn't drop dead from the first round, they'd do a second, more targeted one. After this second day of radiation, he would wait a month and do an MRI to see if it was effective at shrinking his tumours.

Layton was always tired, but the steroids rarely gave him the luxury of proper sleep. If he had a good night's rest, it felt like he could hold on to his short-term memory a bit better than he could on the days when he didn't sleep well. At one oncologist appointment, he learned that surgery might be an option. No one had ever said that before: "Oh, by the way, we can probably take those things out." The issue was that the radiation had killed some of the tumour cells and if those dead cells were still in his brain, they would have to be removed.

When I asked him if he'd noticed any behavioural changes, he thought hard and then said Candace was the person to direct that question to. She'd probably say he was more sensitive, more touchy, he guessed. He'd certainly become more self-conscious about his looks. Layton's gaunt Gerson-era face was replaced with a plumper one. The hollows in his cheeks filled in, and the area joining his chin to his neck lost its sharp definition. At first it appeared these were signs of health returning, but in fact it was the work of the steroids. He continued to plump up so much, developing a round belly, a hump on his back, and a chubby face, that for a month he refused to video chat with me, to go out to see friends. Before, he'd manipulated photos of himself with an app called Fatify to see what he'd look like if he were chubby. Now he was horrified by how his own reflection in the mirror so closely resembled those renderings.

Since the radiation began, he'd had a habit of blaming a lot on "peanut butter brain" or "pbb" as he liked to refer to it in emails. He'd deploy the term when he misremembered what kind of neurological condition a TV character had (it was Alzheimer's, not Parkinson's), or when he asked a question and realized, when someone was giving him the answer, that he'd asked that same question an hour earlier. Once, he sent me a card, peanut butter smeared on the inside. The oil leaked through the envelope, and when I saw the grease stain and his return address, I knew immediately what it was. Sometimes, he'd feel so terrible about forgetting things that the people around him became anxious, quick to reassure him it was okay. Phil liked to turn it into a joke about his own aging mind. "Oh, I can't remember anything either!" he'd say with a forced chuckle. Layton was at peak operating capacity on weekdays, during the daytime. By evening, his brain was spent. On Saturdays and Sundays, with Finn and Candace at home and much more activity around the house, he also was drained faster than usual.

Soon, doctors began weaning him off steroids, switching him to one pill every day. The week before Finn's second birthday, in August, Layton went off steroids completely. By the end of that month, he still weighed 175 pounds, more than he'd weighed in his life, but his face had slimmed considerably. He'd also quit Gerson completely—no more transitional juices or enemas. More than the lifted toll on him, he was pleased his mother would be relieved of all her work and get to reclaim her day.

five

Until this point, everyone always said Finn took after Candace the most: he had her turned-up nose and wide face and his eyes took the same shape as his mother's when he smiled. But now, Layton was delighted to see strange little traces of himself in his son. Sometimes, he'd have what Layton had come to call "excited spasms," when he'd stand on the tips of his toes and jump as high as he could, spin around in circles, and then collapse on the couch.

Finn was only a toddler, but Layton already felt pressure to let his son know he was in a household that would accept him regardless of his sexual preferences or gender identity. "Hey, it's cool if you're into dudes," Layton wanted to tell this little boy, who was still dressed by his mother every morning and spoke in a mix of English and his own invented toddler language. But each day that passed, it was intriguing for Layton to watch the way his son seemed particularly drawn to the young girls at his daycare, how he behaved differently with them than with the little boys. One of Layton's friend's daughters, who was roughly Finn's age, was a tough girl: she'd walk around like a tank, pushing anyone who stood in her path. Finn would stand back and watch her with his hands clasped behind his back, not saying a word but staring in shy admiration. Seeing this side of his son pleased Layton because it reminded him of himself. Finn was also as finicky as Layton was about nighttime routines: he needed all the lights out and for the temperature in his room to be perfect. When Layton was tending to his son's fussy needs, he would occasionally get frustrated, but would then recognize this was a sign of heredity—a direct link between himself and Finn—and his mood would lighten.

After an afternoon family trip to the park one day, Layton told Finn it was time to head home and asked him if he wanted to go on the slide one last time or make a move. Finn went quiet, not answering his father, and calmly stretched out on the ground, lying still for a full minute. The way his body was splayed, it looked like a crime scene—all that was missing was the chalk outline. In the past, he'd thrown tantrums, so this odd behaviour worried his parents.

"There's gotta be something wrong with him," Candace whispered to Layton.

Layton crouched down, putting his face just inches in front of Finn's, and asked in a quiet voice, "What's going on, man?"

Finn looked back at Layton and smiled devilishly—a look that to Layton said, *I own you.* It was a look Layton was certain he'd flashed his parents many times when he was a kid, too.

Layton almost wished he'd taken this turn for the worse earlier, when Finn was still nursing and co-sleeping with Candace, when the boy's mother was his entire world, when it wasn't really even clear if he knew Layton to be his father. Now, Finn had come to expect his dad's company. On some evenings, Layton would lie on the ground in the living room with his head resting on a pillow. Finn would come by and plop his small butt on Layton's forehead and play with his wood blocks or a maze and Layton would melt, wanting no other role in that moment than to serve as his son's chair.

Because creating lists was in her blood, Candace had made one at the beginning of the summer: they'd go to the petting zoo, they'd do a road trip to P.E.I., they'd go to the drive-in to watch a summer blockbuster. It felt like they were living their lives now, even though they knew the outcome they faced was so bleak. As the weeks passed, Candace ticked most items off her summer list. Layton took Finn to the park to fly a kite. The family journeyed to the beach together, where Candace and Finn took a dip in the water while Layton snapped photos from the shore—it seemed wild to Layton that a year and a half ago, such a simple activity would have been impossible without making a few juices to take with them. Still, even though Layton had the freedom to leave the home base, it was where he was most content. On one Sunday evening, the best he could remember, he and Candace sat in the backyard blowing bubbles to their favourite soundtrack: their son giggling.

On Finn's second birthday, both sets of grandparents came to the house, where pictures of characters from *Thomas the*

Tank Engine were plastered on the walls and balloons and streamers filled the living room. Candace baked a typical Candace cake—free of artificial sweeteners—for Finn, who still didn't really know much about refined sugar. The sweetest things he ate were the healthy granola bars Irma gave him, and after each bite, his eyes would light up, the small amounts of cane sugar having reached his pleasure receptors—like Layton's did after eating sweets post-Gerson.

Finn received a batting tee, a bat, and a ball for his birthday, but when the family went outside, all he wanted was to watch Irma throw the ball to Layton and for Layton to hit it. As a result of his treatment and being out of practice, Layton's hand–eye coordination was abysmal. At first, he thought it would be easy to hit home runs with these toys made for toddlers, but after swinging wildly and missing so many times, he could tell Finn was enjoying his failure just as much, so he began missing on purpose, clownishly performing the action, to watch Finn reliably crack up as his plastic bat failed to connect with the ball.

At the end of August, Layton got the results of his latest scan post-radiation: there were now twelve tumours. Two, which were small and on his lungs, were new, but he wasn't too concerned about them. The biggest brain tumours had shrunk or at least stalled in growth, but the smaller ones had grown bigger. If the smaller ones continued growing, his medical team might consider targeted radiation, his oncologist told him, something they would decide after seeing the results of his next MRI in a month.

Layton's doctors had put him on a new drug—a much

improved version of what he'd been offered by Dr. Davis two years earlier but that he'd ultimately rejected in favour of Gerson. There were concerns it might not get past the blood–brain barrier, but at this point, they still wanted to give it a shot—even though it cost twenty thousand dollars a month (which was mercifully funded by the government). Layton tolerated this new drug much better than he had Interferon, but he had little hope of it doing anything besides buying him a few more months than he'd otherwise have. At this time in his life, those months felt worth it.

He'd told his closest friends what had happened, that this cancer had now set up residence in his brain, but the world outside still didn't know. Most had no clue he had cancer, period. He wasn't sure how to respond to the clueless couples who still contacted him through his website, asking if he would photograph their weddings the following summer. (*Hey, sorry I can't shoot your big day. I'll be dead by then.*) He contemplated shutting the whole site down, which was hugely disappointing because he was halfway finished with a redesign that would never see the light of day. He'd not shot a wedding since 2013, but closing up shop still felt like a big step. He tried to see the positive in it: if he cared so much, that must be a sign he'd chosen the perfect job, right?

Feeling a new sense of urgency, Layton now spent his days fixated on curating a collection of items for his son to have after he was gone—the Finn Box. It was a lidded square box with a gorgeous grain and substantial weight that made it seem like the sort of heirloom that had been passed down through the family for several generations. In fact, Layton had scoured the internet for the perfect item and custom-ordered this vessel with a small metal plate engraved with his son's name. He constantly edited and re-edited it in a desperate search for the perfect, stylish set of objects that he wanted to serve as a stand-in for him growing old with Finn. The idea initially seemed simple enough, but he soon felt overwhelmed by the assignment. First, he included a music box that played "You Are My Sunshine," a model of a VW van, family photo prints, a lifelike model of a turtle, some iron-on patches, a medal he'd won in a running event, and several little letters he wrote to Finn, sealed in kraft paper envelopes. He eventually ran out of room, which meant that every time he discovered a new thing to add—old writings or a cloth pencil case or the fake University of Alberta Bachelor of Sociology diploma he'd bought online to score a job teaching English in South Korea— he'd have to take something out. The overflow from the box eventually found a home in a backpack: a wool cap, a set of pencils engraved with Finn's name, a grey hoodie like the ones Layton wore in rotation, a water bottle. What began as a journal to be neatly contained inside the box turned into a full-fledged scrapbook with photos and long, folded letters affixed to the pages with washi tape. Finn was already playing with it: sometimes he'd wander into his parents' room and sit on the bed with Layton. He'd pull things out of the box, rip up shreds of paper, dismantle the camper van while Layton cringed and then laughed. The contents were meaningless to young Finn now, but would they have significance to him when he was ten? Fifteen? The project was simple, and that was precisely the problem—it never felt quite complete.

"It's never enough. I need to put in more. What else can I do? What else can I do?" he complained to Candace.

She believed an assortment of things wouldn't come close to helping Finn understand the man his father was, but she knew this project was something Layton needed to do for his own sanity. There were times when the single-minded obsession to curate these objects prompted arguments between them, and she learned after a while to tell him what he wanted to hear. Layton was never one to take anyone's opinion anyway—what he was actually seeking wasn't her advice but her encouragement. It wasn't worth the fight for her to do anything but what he expected.

Their relationship felt permanently mired in tension now. Layton was longing to get back to the point where he and Candace could fight about stupid things again—these days, it seemed like they were always bickering and the cuts could be deep. Layton wondered if he was being extra-sensitive, reacting in a way that didn't suit the nature of his suffering. Candace wondered sometimes if these fights would be happening at all if Layton was healthy. It was frustrating, too, that she so often had to be the bigger person. She wanted to hold on to the anger sometimes, until he made the move to resolve things, but she knew she couldn't wait him out indefinitely. So after a squabble, she'd leave the room, and when she came back, it was like a reset button had been pressed—ill feelings vaporized, like they'd never had a fight in the first place.

Candace would occasionally suggest, like she had before, that Layton see a therapist. But with his various projects under-way, Layton had something to distract him from dwelling on his feelings. Why would he want to go and sit down with someone who would excavate all the bad stuff that was below the surface? If he was a horrible person or really difficult to live with, he reasoned, he'd put his ego aside and see somebody, but he didn't think he was, so it didn't feel necessary. If Layton wasn't game, then Candace had to do something for herself.

For months, she had wanted to switch positions at the health insurance company where she worked. She'd been processing short-term disability cases for years, but thought it was time to change to handling the long-term ones instead. She knew there was support from her bosses to make the change, but doing so would require spending several months in the office to learn her new responsibilities, and it wasn't possible to take it on when she was working from home for long stretches, looking after Layton. Getting fulfillment at work would have to wait. Instead, Candace began taking a yoga class, and that hour away was the perfect way to decompress.

Layton realized at this time that he could no longer live in his cocoon of secrecy about his health. It had been more than a year since he'd disappeared off Facebook. He thought about how he didn't want Finn's impression of him to be based only on Candace's or his parents' memories. There should be a richer picture. There were people he'd known decades ago, when he was in school or for a few months when working overseas, who had come to shape who he was and had understood pieces of him that his family didn't. He wanted Finn to know those pieces. And so, with much trepidation, he outed himself on Facebook.

hello friends.

did i ever tell you about the time i had a terminal illness?

. . .

*awkward pause ending in three, two, one.

there, that wasn't so bad. like pulling off a band-aid.

very long story short i've got multiple inoperable brain tumours caused by melanoma, a cancer that was originally diagnosed after the removal of a sketchy mole on my back about five years ago. the particulars of my illness will be shared in more detail at some point in the future, just not today. today i have a small favour to ask of you if you're up for it.

outside of navigating the obvious logistics of our current situation, one important focus has been curating a little wooden box of mementos for my two-year-old son, finn. photographs, letters, illustrations, a journal, that sort of thing. i've spent a lot of time thinking about my son growing up without a father and more specifically what types of tangible things i can leave him that will have some genuine meaning to him in ten, twenty, thirty years down the road. it's been a complicated but therapeutic process, the challenge of thinking about what to leave someone who means so much to you but who may not have any real memories of you when he grows up, outside of pictures and stories from friends and family. they say telling stories is more engaging than giving advice, so that's kind of been my focus in my writings to finn. stories from my childhood, work, school, passions, parenthood, love. topics i hope trigger some relatable thoughts on his own experiences/opinions/curiosities as he grows into his own skin. i'd like to think that when you're figuring out who you are, it's nice to know where you came from. half of you, anyway.

i'd also like him to know a little bit about his dad from outside of my own perspective, from the people i've had the opportunity to spend time with while i was here.

that's where the favour comes in.

your mission, should you choose to accept it, is to record a two-minute (or less) video story from a particular time/place/experience we shared together. nothing fancy, just a memory that might stick out in your mind. unbecoming and/or inappropriate memories are welcome, in fact encouraged. i'm not looking for anything overly sanitary, sympathetic or praise-worthy here, to be clear. if i got piss-drunk and took a shit in your backyard one summer night when we were teenagers, say so. unfiltered stories are the best kinds of stories if you ask me. it's your call, really.

i don't know. i don't know what i'm expecting from this, it's an experiment, but if you're up for it, it might be fun, and i really appreciate it for what it's worth. i'll bet future finn does too.

a two-minute (horizontal, pretty please) video recorded on a phone generates a file size of about 20mb, close to the max limit for emailing, so sticking under that mark is probably the easiest way of delivering, if that's ok. i'll gather the files and put them in his box on a usb stick that will most likely be obsolete in six months. he'll be watching youtube videos via a chip embedded in his eyeball by the time he sees these and i'm totally ok with that. jealous, but ok. this request will self-destruct in let's say, how about two weeks from today?

. . .

let's not pull that band-aid off again.

*nervous laugh.

thank you in advance, friends. one million thank-you's to be exact.

big love from our little gang.

l.

bonus friend points: have you or someone close to you lost/ grown up without a father? are you interested in sharing any insight on your experience with me? do you have any suggestions that might have helped/help you navigate that journey a little easier that i might be able to implement now ahead of time? shoot me an email and i'll respond with at least ten high-fives in return.

ok, good talk.

A month later, there was another request.

this box.

some days it consumes me.

it sits on a chair in the corner next to my bed where i spend the majority of my days resting. resting and thinking, an unreasonable amount of thinking most days. i arrange and rearrange the box's contents obsessively, sorting and re-sorting letters and photos and cards and keepsakes, trying my best to make it perfect, wondering what might stick out to him, what will catch his eye, in this box and in his future.

it's all a mystery, to me anyway.

i have no idea what the future holds for this little giant I've had the privilege of getting to know over the last two years. it scares me that i won't be around to share in his journey, but i try to focus that energy back into the box, and in the projects i hope will help him along the way. ideally, i'd love to be able to draft a handwritten note for every conceivable hardship he may come across, but i can't, that's impossible. life never seems to play out as predictably as we'd like it to, anyway. i don't know what he'll have to face, i just hope he has a happy life. good friends, an appetite for adventure and a career he's genuinely passionate about.

it took me a while to find that career for myself, but it seems in retrospect, my early working days kind of evolved through pure happenstance, through starting and quitting and starting and quitting over and over again. twenty-five jobs between high school and my early thirties to be exact.

sometimes i wonder where i would have ended up had my experiences been a little different, had i taken the opportunity to meet folks from different backgrounds

and disciplines early on. folks who were creative and
content and still able to pay the bills. i wonder the same
about finn. at two it's obvious he's going to grow up to
be an excavator-driving human-train hybrid handyman
by day and a salsa dancing mixed martial artist by night.
who knows though, right? it's still early days.

so i have an idea. it came from the dimly lit lightbulb corner
of my brain that still won't quit flickering, so it might be
a stupid one. your job right now is to tell me "everything
is ok layton, your brain is not melting out of your ears
and by god this idea just might work." the job doesn't pay
much but benefits include poking me gently with a stick
the day i wake up convinced i'm blanche from the golden
girls. a fair trade-off.

sooo, wanna help?

sweet.

do you love what you do as a career or hobby? are you
(mostly) stoked to go to work every day? would you be
interested in passing along some of your knowledge and
enthusiasm to my son in a decade or two from now? nice
one. i'm going to go ahead and call this the "it takes a village"
project, mostly because i can't think of a cooler name for
it right now. this will be a kind of future, one-time mini-
mentorship program. without borders. a few hours or an
afternoon spent with finn sharing your passion and giving
him a glimpse into something he might not have thought
of pursuing before. he's a sponge, friends, water him. talk
about how it feels to really love what you do, then show

him. i don't care if you're an engineer, carpenter, bartender, nurse, piano player, teacher, photographer, car salesman or escort. if you're up for volunteering a few hours of your time someday in the future i'd be totally grateful for it, finn too.

the logistics of getting in touch with people ten or fifteen years from now will still need to be ironed out, but if you're interested in sharing your passions (pedophiles: be warned you'll be sniffed out early and have your penises removed in short order) simply email your contact details and the skill-set you'd like to introduce finn to below:

name:

email:

phone:

address:

passion:

. . .

thanks so much, friends. let's show this kid a good time.

l.

Now that he'd published both his grim diagnosis and his callout for the Village Project on Facebook, Layton had received an onslaught of private messages—many from strangers who had come across his posts when their friends had shared them.

One person revealed that their father had died when they were small and all they had left was a pair of scissors, which they treasured. Then, of course, were old friends sharing terrible pictures of Layton from high school—glossy 4x6 prints with the date in red in the corner, which had been scanned or photographed with a mobile phone.

The responses Layton never tired of were the ones that came from people who said they were now going to get a mole checked out or have a screening at a dermatologist's office. But there were plenty of others that left him unsure of how to respond.

So many of them were well-intentioned, but the last thing Layton was seeking was new friendship at this stage of his life. He loved hearing stories from others who had cancer, and he had endless wells of empathy for them, but he didn't like that it felt as though they were coming to him for guidance. What made him qualified to give anyone advice?

Then there were what he classified as the "ghost" responses: where the individual clearly had no clue what to say, so they didn't say anything at all. One old friend from high school had ghosted him, he thought, but then sent an email one day with well-meaning but very much unwelcome naturopathic suggestions: eating freshly grated hot peppers daily, making a slurry with organic raw honey and heaps of grated ginger, using Frankincense and cannabis oil, or switching to the ketogenic diet—which the friend said would starve the cancer cells.

One woman he knew from school but hadn't spoken to in more than a decade sent him a note with the subject line "Farewell"—as though he would be dead the next day. She later told him she had children herself and that her greatest wish for them was "to have both their parents together as they grow up." *What was the point of such a message?* he wondered. To keep himself from firing off an honest reply, he'd rant about these messages to Candace or close friends.

He never quite understood what people meant when they constantly reminded him that he was brave. Brave in what sense? It wasn't like he had a choice in what life had served him. He was trying to keep living a little, in the same way he assumed everyone else in his position would. Making it through years of cancer treatment wasn't brave. Nor were all his foolhardy trips around the world. The bravest thing Layton thought he'd done was shoot weddings. You never knew what would happen once you showed up, if your gear would fail, if the bridesmaids would hate you, if the parents would sabotage some part of the event. Every morning before he left for a wedding, as he double-checked his gear and got into his car, his butt clenched in both anticipation and dread.

The most unexpectedly moving reply Layton got was from Eve, the mother of his childhood friend Liam, a woman who knew loss better than anyone else Layton had met. When Layton was nine, the Reids went to England for the summer to see Phil's family, and when they returned, Willie learned from a neighbour that Liam had been struck and killed by a drunk driver. The tragedy ran deeper: Eve's husband had died from cancer not long before that.

When he got older, Willie asked Layton if he ever thought about Liam. "Every single day," he said. And Eve knew. On her birthday, months after Liam's death, Layton asked his mother if they had a basket and she found him one. He stole some money from her purse and biked to the supermarket to buy a few things to fill it with and then continued on to

Eve's house, put the basket on her doorstep, rang the doorbell, and hid.

Eve opened the door to find a basket filled with a chocolate
bar, a chestnut, a flower, and other items Layton had carefully
chosen. She looked up to see who had made the delivery and
caught a glimpse of Layton's skinny frame hiding around the
side of the house. But she maintained the illusion she hadn't
seen him, and his act of kindness became an annual birthday
tradition, when he would deliver pizza to her house, or an
assortment of candies, or movie vouchers. When he became
too sick to do these drop-offs himself, he had Willie deliver a
bottle of wine.

That summer, Eve's other son, Sean, got married and she
emailed Layton a few photos from the event. He replied with
a candid question: had her husband left anything for the family, knowing he would die? Her response soothed him more
than any other he received.

1) I know that whatever you leave will never seem to you to be
enough: at the same time these gifts will go farther than you
think. The photos and letters you mentioned will help more
than you can know so make sure they are encased in material
that will withstand lots of handling.

2) The time you are spending with Finn now has lasting value.
I spent many years in Early Childhood Education. The long-
term research showed conclusively that these early years have
significant impact in later life.

3) There is definitely some pain in growing up without a dad. It seems to be part of the human condition that many kids experience some pain. It is also part of the human condition that in spite of, during and even because of that, they will still experience joy. His pain will come from a place of knowing his dad is a great and loving presence with whom he wants regular and physical contact. He will figure out how to relate to you in his new reality. Yes, sometimes it will bring pain, but you will continue to bring him real moments of joy.

4) Sean remembers and thinks about his father every day. Since he was 10 when Patrick died he has a good store of memories. However, his dad's memory is also largely based on the adults that were around him. Even at his wedding there was a space created for his dad. You have a great team. Your parents have been so present during this part of your life. They are going to provide support for Finn and continue his connection to you. You can count on that.

5) One thing I remember about Patrick is that he had trust in the future, even one without his physical presence. It was genuine. It kind of gave us some confidence to move forward. And he was right. He knew we would find our way.

6) I'm sure you know that your greatest asset in this concern is Candace. I'm not saying that any of this is easy or straightforward but pat yourself on the back for choosing such a capable and loving wife and mother. She will be his champion, and I can think of few people who would measure

up as well to such a task. And people will be kind to her and
want to help.

So Layton, the gist of what I'm saying is that you have actually
already done all the tangibles and intangibles that I can think of.
If you are here for the short or long term, you have your people
and plans in place to nurture and protect your son. I know it
doesn't feel complete from your view but I think that is an
inevitable part of parenting. We always think we could be doing
something more or better. Clearly, at least to my eyes, you are
already doing "more" and "better."

The note gave Layton confidence. Sean experienced a longing
for his father from time to time, it seemed, but also felt curiosity
and a connection to him. Layton followed up with more questions and she replied.

Hey there, good to hear from you. I have a confession. After
I wrote my response to you I took your question to Sean because
he is my go-to sounding board person. I trust his judgement a
lot. I hope this is not a betrayal of your trust but I also thought
he could offer the child perspective. He had some suggestions
that I would never have thought of.

1) Tape/video with voice: He said he thought in addition to
Finn having your words in writing he might also benefit from
a video or something which would also include your voice,
mannerisms, gestures—some sound or visual information.
As a teen Sean started trying to figure out more about his dad

and if he had any of the same traits. And he does. They share an insane laugh.

2) Photos: Sean wishes that he had a few good photos of just him and Patrick. He wondered if, because you are the main photographer in your family, there may not be many of just you and Finn.

3) Milestones: When Sean hit some milestones—becoming a teenager, a young adult, marriage, becoming a parent (well, not yet but maybe some day)—he wanted to know what these experiences were like for Patrick. What were his hopes, dreams, thoughts, fears, at that time? What advice, if any, could he have offered? You might be able to write on those topics and have them saved for the milestone events in Finn's life.

4) Personality: This came out of a discussion Sean had with a friend whose dad also passed when she was quite young. They both felt that they wanted more information on their father's personality. What people shared with them over the years was all the good stuff so they ended up with an idealized version of Dad. They loved and appreciated that but also want the true grit, as in: what were Dad's fears? What mistakes did he make? What caused him to get angry? Vices? Grudges? All the guts to go with the glory. I wondered about this because parents generally don't want to reveal their weaknesses to their children. But for Sean it addresses the question of "who was my father as an adult" and "what sort of adult relationship would I have with him?" None of this was going to cause him to love his dad less or to judge him

*harshly. He just wanted to know him more deeply. Heaven
knows Sean has had a lifetime-full of my flaws and weaknesses
and still maintains he loves me, so I think it's a safe reveal.*

•

Now that his secret was out, a lot of people would ask to visit
Layton, and he usually turned them down. Life was already
both exhausting and fleeting. It felt selfish, but if he had energy,
he wanted to spend it with his son. What he did think he owed
people, though, were updates. More posts. He had let them
in to a degree, and it seemed cruel not to keep them abreast of
what was going on. There was a kind of responsibility now to
continue being candid with this concerned audience. One night
at dinner, Candace asked, "How do you feel about people
knowing all this stuff?" And it gave Layton pause. Candace was
antsy about their relatively private life being so public now,
especially since Layton's business address—which was their
home address—could be found online. He gave in and took
down the address, but never quite understood Candace's worry,
in the same way he never understood why she was uncomfortable walking home alone at night.

Sometimes, Layton worried that he hadn't chosen the right
words to articulate what he wanted to say—that people might
misconstrue his posts, or think they were too dark. He tried to
detach himself from what he wrote and to imagine reading it
from the perspective of a friend whom he hadn't been in touch
with for a while. It was like catching his reflection in the win-
dows of a building without expecting to.

will i be in pain? will i feel alone? will i be brave? will i find
peace? will candace be with me? will she be ok? will she
know how much i'll miss her? will she remember to pay the
power bill? will she sell the house? will she find another
partner? will he be good enough for her? will he be good
enough for my son? will she get remarried? will she still
want to be buried next to me if she remarries? will finn miss
me? will he be happy? will he look like me when he's older?
will he be bullied? will he be the bully? will he be kind to
others? will he find love? will he find a career he's passionate
about? will he be sensitive in the same ways his dad was?
will he be good to his mom? will he play pickup basketball
at oxford once in a while? will he stay close with his
grandparents? will he still remember me in a few years?
will he know how much i loved him? will he love me in
return? will he be in pain? will he feel alone? will he be
brave? will he find peace?

   Xo

                              •

It was like Layton and Candace had lived a dozen lifetimes in the
five years since they'd been married. When she'd worn her strapless gown and he his suspenders and they'd exchanged vows,
they weren't yet homeowners or dog owners or parents or a
couple trying to figure out how to live when one of them was
so close to death. Getting to their five-year anniversary, Layton
decided earlier in the year, was an occasion they had to mark in
a big way.

Their friend Evan, who was also a wedding photographer, spent a few hours at the house on the day of their anniversary. When he arrived, Layton and Candace were wearing un-intentionally matching outfits: grey hoodies and jeans. It took the two of them a while—interrupted by a toddler crying session—to wrangle Finn into his formalwear for the day: black trousers, a blue Oxford shirt, and a navy striped bowtie, which Candace carefully fastened around his neck. Taking turns looking after their son, Layton and Candace disappeared to their rooms to change. Layton emerged in an untucked shirt that matched his son's, the first pair of formal pants he'd worn in years, a grey tie, and navy sneakers. Candace, meanwhile, came out in a nude sleeveless dress with black lace overlay. As the trio stood in front of their house, laundry drying outside on a rack to the left of the front door, they looked like they might be on their way to a friend's wedding, but the main event that day was to take place right there on the front stoop.

The same justice of the peace who had married them five years earlier arrived to direct the ceremony, this time with only Evan, his wife, and Finn as witnesses. The couple had written new vows that they read to each other, ones that car-ried even more gravity than the last ones. And then everyone retreated to the house for cupcakes and Finn played with his trains on the kitchen floor as the adults chatted in the next room, putting levity back into the day.

When I visited Layton that same month, it was the first time we didn't eventually end up in his room. It was the first time he wasn't feeling so weak that he needed to lie down in bed as we spoke. Despite this, his outlook was bleak.

As he stood outside, collecting acorns with Finn, he told me, "I don't think I'll survive the winter," like some character from a period piece who was afraid that his body, so ravaged from whooping cough or scarlet fever, might not have the strength to make it through the season.

Even his smallest goals seemed out of reach. Would he get to see the new *Star Wars* film that was coming out at the end of the year? Probably not. Would the last movie he ever saw at a drive-in theatre remain *American Wedding*? It seemed likely.

In early December, just before Finn's third Christmas, Layton got some good news from his doctor. The new drug he was on had gotten rid of a few of his brain tumours, which was a pretty uncommon outcome—an early Christmas gift. But still, he told his mother not to broadcast the news because he knew he couldn't handle a tsunami of "you're cured" or "don't give up" emails. It was nice to know that his scans reflected how much better he was feeling. His bald head was now sprouting a layer of light blond fuzz, a sign of returning health.

Now he needed to find a new set of goals. With Gerson, they were built in: he'd worked hard to follow the treatment plan perfectly in order to get a clean scan. Clean scans were off the table now, but he still craved some kind of structure to his days, to his life. Running had always given him the ultimate feeling of control over his body, and for the first time in more than two years, he laced up his sneakers with the aim of getting back that feeling.

It wasn't easy—Layton was in the worst shape of his life. His body was completely deconditioned from two years of inactivity and he was missing part of his lung from the previous year's surgery. The first excursion was a granny shuffle around the block, during which he brought his iPod and ran the stopwatch on it. Seven minutes, 37.54 seconds. He used to be able to run multiple *kilometres* in that time. He knew he could build himself back up while he was still alive, or at least try to.

The week after Christmas, he had a cold and came to terms with the fact that he would have to miss the annual Herring Cove Polar Bear Dip again, which happened every year on New Year's Day. It was a tradition that he knew, intellectually, was absurd, but one he still felt drawn to. In his blood, in his bones, he felt it was something he needed to do. Though he'd pushed his body to extremes over the last few years in treating his cancer, what could be a more electrifying physical experience than running into the frigid Atlantic Ocean? A bigger test of what the human body could withstand?

He went out for drinks that week with a friend who brought along one of his friends. As they were leaving, the friend of a friend, a woman, who learned Layton's story that night, turned to him.

"You know, I think you're going to live longer than you think you are," she said, staring into his eyes.

"Really?" Layton asked.

"Yeah, I have ESP," she said.

And then he asked a question he'd never once wanted to ask his doctors: "How long?"

"Maybe two years," she said.

Layton smiled to himself on the drive home. Who was this woman? What proof was there that she knew anything? It didn't matter. He liked what she had to say.

On New Year's Eve, Candace and Layton were in bed by 8:30. There was no need to stay up till midnight since he knew he'd be waking up the next morning and could greet 2016 then. And maybe he would do the same for 2017, too.

•

With the new year came new parental responsibilities, like toilet training Finn. It reminded Layton of training Gracie, except that Finn seemed smarter than his trainer and could manipulate him at every move—but he still couldn't figure out that he was pissing until he was finished pissing.

Layton received the results of a chest and stomach CT—it was clean. He emailed to tell Willie that and she misunderstood. She thought that somehow there had been a scan of his whole body and even the brain tumours were gone. She sent him and Candace a very enthusiastic, manic message of jubilation. Layton, feeling terrible about the miscommunication, clarified that it was the stomach and chest. It was very likely the brain tumours were still there and he'd find out a few weeks later when the MRI results came in. She replied, "Indeed, that's still good, right?"

Snow had piled up several inches on the long driveway and path leading to the front door the day Layton was to find out the results of his MRI. He put on his coat and boots and spent an hour and a half shovelling before he drove to the hospital. Halifax's winters typically dragged on well into March. There would be a few sunny days of melt and rain and then suddenly the temperature would sink below zero, turning puddles into hazards for cars and pedestrians. Then there would be more snow, and before it could melt from the sun it would get rained on, turning into slushy soup. No matter what the results of these scans were, Layton wanted to at least be able to claim he'd survived this winter he'd been certain he wouldn't.

.

Layton did survive the winter, but complications awaited him in the months that followed the thaw. Irma was now renting a place in Halifax, and on Mother's Day, Candace and Layton had planned to head over to her apartment with Finn for brunch. But before her guests arrived, Irma got a call from her daughter: Layton had had a seizure and an ambulance was on the way. This one he felt on one side of his body, which was more terrifying than previous ones when he'd zoned out. A brain CT showed there was swelling on the left side of his brain, so he was told he had to start on steroids again. For Layton, every trip to the hospital felt like dying, but then he was discharged and it was like being born again. Candace decided to take the week off work to spend with him before his next MRI. He wasn't allowed to run on his own anymore, for fear he might have a seizure, so Phil joined him on neighbourhood jogs.

Running while on steroids was hell. The drugs not only changed his body in the most basic sense—they stole the lean muscles from his legs and replaced them with fat deposits; they gave him what a doctor friend told him was "a buffalo hump" on his back—but they also zapped him of his energy. Even jogging a short distance felt like he was trying to sprint through a sea of molasses. But what was important was that now that the fifteen rounds of radiation were over, he could at least do some kind of exercise, even if it felt like ineffective shuffling. It was an achievement for him to be able to run, to be physically active again, to have the mental energy to type emails, to compose Facebook posts, to write letters to Candace and Finn, to see his friends more regularly. To drive to the store to pick up toilet paper, even.

On one scorching day in mid-May, Layton and Phil donned bibs for a race. Instead of Layton leaving his father in the dust like he often had throughout their lives, their roles were now reversed. Phil knew his son would be irritated if he slowed down to meet his pace. The heat made the run more excruciating than others Layton had done, and he felt it more acutely because of the steroids. He experienced only a bit of the runner's high he used to feel after races when he was healthier, but it was eclipsed by something else. This was a different sensation altogether: it was like every part of his body throbbed, his heart pounded dangerously in his chest, his lungs felt ready to collapse, but he had still finished. He had proven that he retained some command over his body that was otherwise rebelling against him.

His next MRI results, which he got in early June, were positive. Unlike what his doctors had assumed, the swelling wasn't brought on by a massive new tumour; they believed it was instead caused by necrosis—the death of a tumour. They'd scheduled another scan for July, and if swelling hadn't subsided by then, they'd consider surgery to remove it. Even dead, the tumour could be a problem.

Layton completed more runs as they came up over the

following weeks, tracking his time like he was building up to a marathon someday. By mid-June, he completed a 5K in twenty-seven minutes, shaving four minutes off his time from his first run since he'd started back up again. He now recalibrated his goals. He was a different man running in a different body. He'd never do a 5K in eighteen minutes again, like he had when he was healthy, but he wanted to see how close he could get.

it's a curious feeling having breasts.

all these years i've fantasized about having a pair of my own, but now that they're here i can't help but think that boobs aren't really all they're cracked up to be, not when you're trying to break a measly twenty-five-minute 5k, anyway.

but alas, here i am. a gimped up knee, a pulled groin, twenty pounds of extra weight, nipples covered in band-aids, and my modest A cups bouncing in the wind to the beat of eminem's eight mile soundtrack, trying to scrounge up enough energy to shuffle around the neighborhood just one more time without coughing up what's left of my lungs.

steroids, it seems, are a cruel but necessary evil. they help keep your brain from swelling up but leave the rest of your body wasted of muscle while replacing it with swollen skin, a puffy body and humps in places humps don't naturally belong. it's gross. i'm gross. but i've said it before and i'll say it again. my decision to run is based solely on the fact that i still can. that's it. i'll keep running until my body says i can't. till it leans over my broken bones and bleeding brain and gently whispers into my one good ear "enough is enough, my love. it's time for you to go now."

this life, the last six years, haven't been easy. some days i've felt like i've been racing against hurdles and have managed to knock over every last one, but i've also discovered a hugely important lesson along the way.

would you like to learn the secret to taking on life's most brutal obstacles?

here it is.

there is no secret. just keep moving, dummy. that's it. physically, figuratively, whatever. my hundred year old grandfather taught me that by walking the equivalent of the circumference of the earth over the course of his lifetime. my father taught me that by running over thirty-seven thousand kilometres since he graduated from high school, and my son teaches me that by digging, sprinting and splashing his way through a seemingly infinite well of energy, and that kid's only three years old.

run. walk. crawl. i don't care. just keep moving forward and you'll eventually get to where you need to go.

i promise.

Xo

•

For a few months in the summer, Layton had to take a break from the 5Ks after he pulled his groin. He was running a different kind of race throughout all this: one against his body's internal clock. He was desperate to fit in as much father–son time as he could this summer, but without feeling like the hours were forced or rushed. Finn was at an age now where he was manipulating his parents in any way he could, but Layton saw things differently than Candace did—it could be hard to be the tough parent when he was overjoyed to have any time with his child. Who wanted to be a disciplinarian? Not that Finn even took him seriously as one. At times, Layton felt like a visitor playing catch-up, trying to earn the trust and respect of his own kid. On most days, he was only a hair above a really good playmate—and happy enough with that.

In most social situations, Finn was still the kid who would stand with his hands clasped behind his back, staring at what was unfolding around him, but once he got comfortable, he'd release his contagious belly laugh, capturing the attention of everyone in the room who had perhaps not noticed his presence earlier. Almost every day, the time after daycare involved a photo session: Finn in a perfectly coordinated Gap Kids outfit, collecting leaves or running laps in the backyard. One June day, before Father's Day, Finn asked Layton, "Daddy, can you put your clamera away?" slurring the word. Layton immediately removed the strap from his neck, wishing he was close enough to the ocean to toss the stupid clunky barrier between him and his son into the water right then. On sunny summer evenings, Finn watered the flowering dogwood tree planted for his father on Father's Day, and Layton watered the Japanese maple planted for his son to commemorate his birth. They spent hours in the backyard blowing bubbles, a mercifully low-energy activity. In July, Layton started to teach Finn how to ride a bicycle with training wheels.

But Candace never felt fully comfortable with Layton and Finn out in the yard without someone else there. She wanted to give Layton the sense that he was the responsible parent looking after his son, but she'd join them outside—even when she was exhausted—or keep watch from the kitchen window.

It was always Candace's evening ritual to get Finn ready for bed, but one night Layton subbed in. Finn resisted as Layton tried to wrangle his son's wriggling body into his cotton pyjamas, kicking and pouting.

"No!" Finn squealed. "Mummy do this!"

"I'm not going to be here forever, buddy," Layton said softly.

He was tired of fighting for parental equality, so he gave in at that moment; Mummy would be the one doing it later, anyhow.

Another evening, Finn vomited in his bed and it was Candace who had to clean it up, since Layton was downstairs, asleep on the couch. But then the next day, Finn didn't go to daycare and Layton felt like he was the parent in charge—even though Candace was working from home. Layton was learning that time was all it took: the more time he spent with Finn, the more time Finn wanted to spend with him, and the more Finn respected him.

one of the weird by-products of being diagnosed with a terminal illness is having to deal with how other people react to it. family, friends, strangers on the street, everyone handles the news differently. navigating those reactions can sometimes be more difficult than taking on the illness itself.

luckily for me, i have one of my best friends in my corner, a boy who couldn't care less about my friends in the attic.

a boy who just wants to have fun, play with trains and grab on his wiener all day. and you know what? i can respect that. i know that when we're together he's not feeling sorry for me or trying to come up with something comforting to say. if he's happy, he'll show me. if he's frustrated, he'll tell me. and if he's hangry, he'll lock candace and i in the kitchen and burn the whole house to the ground.

i think what i'm trying to say here is that he lives in the moment.

he doesn't concern himself with the past or the future, with what may or may not happen next week, or what may or may not happen next year. he just doesn't think about it, and when i'm with him i don't think about it either.

and if you ask me that's the best kind of friend you can have.

Xo

•

Layton had checked off the little box on his driver's licence that said he would donate his body for both transplant and medical research, but, unsettled by the idea of being dissected and then discarded, he decided he'd rather be cremated. It was a depressing subject to research because, in the end, cremation was like any other business transaction. He found one local company that promised to beat the price of any competitor by 10 per cent. How heartwarming.

He didn't want to sit in some stodgy brass urn on his parents' mantle, and so he ordered a tiny puck that looked like a camera lens in profile. It could hold a small portion of ashes for Finn—he had bigger plans for the rest. After the urn arrived in the mail, Layton posted a photo of it on Facebook with a very Laytonesque caption: "i'm a planner." The photos he'd post of Finn often racked up hundreds of likes within an hour, but this one didn't do so well. Many friends responded in horror, but some saw humour in it; Layton was dying and this was what it looked like.

When he was in his twenties, before he was even sick, Layton told his friend Sarah he wanted his ashes divided between seven bags, each assigned to a different friend and a different continent. Each friend would be tasked with taking their designated portion of cremated Layton to their assigned continent and to a country they'd never travelled to before to scatter them. Over the years, he'd modified the dream a little. In one of his Facebook posts, he'd laid out his demands for after his death, one of which was having someone take his ashes to Antarctica. When he put it up, he thought of it as a sort of a narcissistic joke, but a few people, some of them relative strangers, had actually stepped up with serious offers to do it. He immediately regretted posting it. It was moments like this when he understood that he wasn't only writing to his friends, that there were people—people he'd never met—who were deeply invested in his story. It was too much to take these individuals up on their offer; seeing their generosity made him want to shrink away and cut himself off from the world beyond the four walls of his house.

Willie had known from the first phone call back when Layton was in Ottawa, telling her about the mole he'd had removed, that things would not end well for her son. She knew it was likely she would be burying him rather than the other way around. That summer, Willie felt it was time to see a counsellor. At her first appointment, as the minute hand made a full trip around the clock, she simply cried. The next time, the counsellor proposed doing a type of therapy based on eye movement, in which the individual takes a difficult situation or memory and gets to the heart of the trauma by thinking about it in detail. "What was the worst thing for you?" the counsellor asked. "The phone call from Ottawa," Willie answered. She explained she could recall what she was wearing, what time of day it was, where she was sitting—that's how often she'd played and replayed it in her head over the years. The counsellor led her through the memory like it was a train trip, stopping frequently to ask Willie where she was at on this metaphorical journey. Something had changed after that session. Willie still felt sadness when she thought about that call, but not the deep, gut-wrenching kind she'd experienced all those times before.

She felt more ready to accept her son's impending death now, and though she discussed it with Phil on occasion, she always waited for Layton to take the lead on conversations about it. A friend gave her a copy of *When Breath Becomes Air*, the bestselling memoir written by a neurosurgeon with Stage IV lung cancer, with instructions to give it to Layton, but she didn't. She was so protective of him. She was waiting for him to tell her he was ready for these conversations.

One day, when she sat up with him on his bed, Layton mentioned that he'd changed his mind about what he wanted to happen to his remains after he died. Candace had pointed out it might be nice for some of his ashes to be buried some-where nearby.

"Candace really wants a place to take Finn," he told his mother.

"What about beside Granny and Grandpa?" she asked.

"Oh, could I do that?" he said, his eyes lighting up.

Willie beamed. "That would be wonderful!" she said. "They would be so pleased."

When the Reids had travelled to see Willie's parents when Layton was younger and at his wildest, his maternal grand-father had seemed to be the only one who could corral the little spitfire. It seemed appropriate that they'd be neighbours at rest.

.

On a misty Friday morning in July, after leaving Finn at daycare, Layton and Candace set out for New Glasgow, a picturesque Nova Scotia town about 170 kilometres from their home. It was like the east coast road trips they used to take before Layton got sick, though this time Candace was in the driver's seat. They soared down the highway listening to pop music on satellite radio, passing old trees with big canopies and quaint little homes on sprawling parcels of land, and then reached Layton's grand-parents' old house.

The house was now owned by a woman whose wedding Layton had coincidentally shot years earlier. When he was in his twenties, Layton had buried two time capsules in the back-yard and had received permission from his former client to excavate them that day. Candace was in a blue windbreaker, the hood pulled up to protect her hair from the frigid wind whipping through the trees. She wandered all over the moist underbrush, her white sneakers sinking slightly into the soft, wet earth, wielding a borrowed metal detector—the kind Layton had only ever seen amateur gold prospectors use on the beach in sitcoms. No luck. Later, they targeted their digging, unearthing pieces of scrap metal and bits of an old bed frame but no time capsules.

On the way home, they stopped at the Crossroads Market to pick up homemade cinnamon buns for Layton's parents and sat down in a Swiss Chalet to have quarter-chicken dinners for lunch—his with fries, hers with a baked potato and steamed vegetables on the side. It was the kind of food loaded with fat and sodium that Layton had loved when he was younger. He relished the meal.

But before that lunch stop, they detoured to the cemetery where Layton's grandparents were buried. It wasn't actually a detour but the primary reason for the excursion—Layton had to sandwich it between a wacky time capsule excavation mission and a diner lunch to give it some semblance of a fun road trip with Candace. Layton had visited his grandparents' burial site before, but not since the cancer had returned. It was quiet and peaceful and every adjective one would reach for when describing a cemetery in the middle of the day.

They quietly ambled through the tidy rows of plots, studying the other tombstones to get an idea of what style Layton might like. He knew immediately he didn't want the ostentatious kind that loudly asserted its presence and seemed to be in competition with others—he wanted something small and humble. After a few laps, he realized the ones he was most drawn to were the oldest, their edges smoothed down by wind and precipitation and time, the once sharp lettering on them now softened and occasionally difficult to read.

He and Candace talked about something that had been on Layton's mind a lot: whether Candace would want to be buried beside Layton or somewhere else—maybe beside her second husband, if she decided to remarry. It wasn't an easy visit for Candace, who had spent the week ticking off other terrible items, like revising their wills, from the to-do list. All these tasks pushed her to come to grips with her husband's impending death. But she didn't have much time to stew in that feeling.

Layton quickly adjusted the settings on his DSLR, and handed it to her. Then he curled up in front of his grandparents' shared tombstone, pretending he was a corpse. In truth, he looked like an overgrown toddler at nap time: his hands stacked under his right cheek, knees folded towards his chest, the seat of his grey sweatpants soaked from the wet grass. As Candace rolled her eyes and pressed down on the shutter, Layton, his eyes squeezed shut, smiled. He was still alive enough to play dead.

I remember staying at my parents' house, I was sleeping
in the attic, he was down in the spare room, in the middle of
the night my mom would be up with him trying to calm him
down. He'd wake up thinking he was in New Glasgow, or he
needed to be somewhere else, or that someone had broken
in and stolen things from the house. That moment it really
hit me how much of my parents' lives had been sacrificed to

take care of him, not just in the end, a good part of his later years really.

I had a lump in my throat, like, ok, the grandpa we knew is no longer with us, that's ok.

Then early the next morning, back off to Ottawa, I said goodbye to him like I had done many times before. We stood in the hallway with my mother and for a second it was like his mind had come back to say goodbye one last time.

Completely lucid. Eyes locked.

Ok, Layton, I'll see you next time he smiled.

Alright grandpa, see you next time.

No thank you for being an inspiration in my life, no sorry for not spending a lot of time with you in my teens or taking enough photos of you over the years.

Just . . . see you next time.

And I walked out the door.

Dad phoned me in Ottawa the morning he died as I was on my way out the door again to run a road race I had foolishly signed up for without any real training. After some time, I decided to go ahead and do it anyway . . . and ended up running a sub 40-minute 10k for the first time in years. I am by no means a religious, or even spiritual person, but I've no doubt he was with me that day.

And then we had his funeral. And just like that there was nothing left.

Just memories of him. And his home.

As these things usually work out my parents were in charge of selling the house and all of its property. They ended up negotiating with a young spit-fire by the name of Courtney, and her newly engaged partner Eric. They had big plans for the house. A new start for them and a new start for that space. It was exciting for everyone involved. My mother, like mothers do, told Courtney her son was a wedding photographer. I rolled my eyes like I usually do when mom tries to pimp me out, but this time it worked out. After a brief meeting in Halifax we were all set to go. I'd be shooting a wedding in my grandpa's backyard.

What a trip.

•

A few weeks after settling on where his ashes would be buried, it was time for Layton to go headstone shopping. He fantasized about something radical, the kind of piece that could be part of a MoMA exhibition, but knew the good church-attending people of Thorburn might not like having something so high-concept in their space. He even thought of finding a large rock and simply having something engraved in that, but Candace dismissed that idea. He couldn't have something too small or people would assume he was a child, or just plain cheap. He'd learned already that he had to consider what others deemed acceptable when it came to making decisions about death. After his trip to the cemetery, he'd posted the photo Candace had taken of him pretending to sleep beside his grandparents' graves on Facebook and had received a few scolding messages. Some said it was disrespectful, others chided him for being so flippant about death. He laughed, knowing these people were simply uncomfortable with how comfortable *he* was with his mortality. Too bad if they couldn't take a joke.

There were a few shops scattered down Bedford Highway, so he hit them all up in one day. Maybe this could be settled before he went home.

The first was the best—there were plenty of examples in the showroom, the saleswoman was kind and answered the endless questions he had.

The second took a much different approach. An employee shoved catalogues at Layton as soon as he stepped through the door and circled the ones that were on sale. He flipped through the pages—was there anything she marked that was less than four thousand dollars? Nope. He promptly handed the catalogues back to the woman, said thank you, and headed out the door, whispering "eat shit" under his breath.

The last place was the worst. The saleswoman was cold, dismissive. When Layton pointed to one headstone he liked and asked if it was available in a smaller size, the woman chuckled to herself. Layton bristled. The terrible thing was that this shop had the nicest headstones, but now, on principle, he couldn't buy them there since this woman had mocked him. It felt like he was shopping at a used car lot for a car he needed but didn't want to buy. He swallowed his annoyance and decided to leave. As he headed out the door, the saleswoman asked who the headstone was for. Layton turned around, smiling like the Cheshire Cat, and told her, "Me. I've got some friends in the attic." She looked confused. "Sorry?" she asked. Layton kept walking, calling over his shoulder. "Friends. In. The. Attic." The door slammed shut behind him.

dear mel.

i hope you don't mind me calling you that. melanoma just sounds so formal, you know? i just thought i'd check in and catch up and let you know how things are going on my end. i feel like we never really get a chance to talk anymore, just the two of us.

finn turned three last month (total rapscallion) and candace is on this big minimalist kick lately. inexplicably, and due in large part to a handful of my cancer-killing crew at the VG, i am, as of today, still upright. what a trip. some days are better than others of course but i guess that goes with the territory, right?

as you're well aware, three of my friends in the attic have bulked up a bit over the summer, so it looks like i'll be in this week for a last ditch effort to see if we can at least keep them at bay before i start having panic attacks in public and pooping in my pants. again. i'm confident i can enjoy a diaper-free existence until at least the end of the year, but what do i know?

all i know is until our paths cross again i just wanted to take a minute to say thank you. genuinely.

i know we've had our differences in the past and i know we've not always seen eye to eye, but i've learned so many lessons i never would have, had we not been introduced a handful of years ago in the back of a sketchy walk-in clinic in downtown ottawa. back where this whole silly adventure began. back when you taught me all the ultra-important rules to remember about this unmistakably messy yet miraculous life of mine.

lessons on perspective, patience, pain and above all, resilience.

i have loved and been loved more in the last few years than i have in the first thirty-five or so of my life and i appreciate things today that i most certainly would have taken for granted the day before we met. most importantly though i've accumulated a ton of cool scars to show finn before i have to eventually squeeze his clammy little hand into mine and remind him to be good to his mummy and hope he remembers just how much i loved him when he's old enough to process this whole shitty nightmare of a situation i've inadvertently put my family through.

so, if we don't get a chance to chat again before you decide enough is enough, just know that i'm grateful for everything you've done for me. i don't know if that was your intention back when we originally met but at the moment that's all i can think about. how you've changed my life, temporarily at least, for the better.

i'll miss you mel, you old magnificent, malignant, murdering masterpiece. thank you once more for giving my family the strength to band together to fight for a cause much bigger than me, and thank you for the opportunity to safely gather my things and say my goodbyes one last time before i hobble proudly off into the sunset, camera in hand and a photo of candace and finn in my back pocket.

yours sincerely, and still alive.

layton reid.

Xo

•

Though Phil had run ahead of his son in the first few 5K races they did together, now he liked to keep pace with him, even if this meant slowing down considerably. At the beginning, the two didn't speak—Layton was always too winded from the exertion—but their bodies found a way to converse each time their hips swung forward and feet hit the asphalt.

Phil's favourite race was the one in Bedford, where he and Layton got completely drenched but stayed on the course, laughing at the absurd lengths they were pushing themselves to. They took a photo at the end on a bench, their legs splayed out, leaning against each other back-to-back for support. Following another run, Layton insisted Candace take a photo of him lying on the ground in front of a tangle of shrubs, his head and arms buried in greenery but the rest of him exposed as though he'd been killed by someone who didn't care to dispose of his body properly. To Layton, it was less about running the races and more about completing them, which is why he needed photographic evidence every time he crossed the finish line.

When he was healthy, he'd be flushed and breathing deeply at the end of a run, but there was always a firmness and confidence in his stride. Now it looked like every metre was a struggle, and that could be difficult for Phil and Candace to witness. Sometimes, they wanted to tell him to take it easy, that he didn't have to finish, but they knew that would only make Layton more determined.

At every medical appointment they attended together, Candace and Layton would have the same conversation. "Is there anything you want to know that I don't want to know?" he'd ask her. If she said yes, Layton would step into the hallway, leaving Candace and the doctor alone. Candace would press them on what it all meant. "How bad is it?" she'd ask. There were points when she thought Layton was doing well because he'd been stable for a few weeks, but was he really?

Layton's oncologist, a much younger doctor who had replaced Dr. Davis after she retired, said there would be warning signs when Layton's death approached—faltering memory, changes in temperament, seizures—and Candace started looking for them, like an amateur coroner trying to do an autopsy in reverse. In Canada, the federal government provides "compassionate care" benefits for people who have a gravely ill family member and must take time off work to look after them. Because the leave time is a maximum of six months, Candace wanted to take full advantage of it as soon as she knew Layton was in that range.

Sometimes at these appointments, Candace and the doctor would be in the room for twenty-five minutes while Layton waited in the hallway. *What does Candace know?* he wondered. *Why does she want to know this?* Afterwards, as they walked through the parking lot, Layton would pepper her with questions. Candace had a terrible poker face, so when she caught him trying to read her expression, she'd pick up her pace.

"Go away!" she'd say, playfully swatting his face with her hand. "You said you didn't want to know, so bugger off."

She was mostly candid with Layton's parents, but at times she wanted to protect them the way she did their son. That August, Willie and Phil took a three-day biking trip in Cape

Breton, and when they returned, they learned that Layton had had several small seizures. Far from being resentful or angry that Candace had withheld this information, they were grateful. What could they have done, anyway? They would've packed up their bikes and needlessly returned home, worrying for their son like they always did.

The increased frequency of seizures was a red flag for Candace, and one day she quietly called her mom, seeking advice. Should she take the six-month compassionate care leave now? Should she wait?

"If I take it now," she told Irma, "Layton's going to think I know something and he's really sick. But if I wait, what if something happens and I don't have that time with him?"

it's monday.

a cool but sunny afternoon. candace and i are in the backyard lounging in our fake red canadian tire adirondack chairs eating lunch while finn naps inside, approximately eight feet from where we're sitting. it's the first time in a long time we've had the opportunity to just take a breath together and try to digest everything that's happened over the last three months while she takes some time off work and we begin to transition into my new and likely last stage of treatment.

it's been a busy and complicated summer and we've done our best to pack in as many adventures as possible, one of which included grand plans of digging up an old time capsule i buried years ago in my grandparents' backyard out in new glasgow. we borrowed a metal detector and everything, but unfortunately no luck. the location of the bounty is still very much a mystery, and to be honest i kind of like the idea of that.

at the moment, with full bellies and the sun on our backs we're starting to feel pretty restful, trying to take advantage of this stolen opportunity to just sit, even if it's only for an hour or so, to close our eyes and relax, side by side, while we do our best to recharge and reconne . . .

ok wait, there she goes.

she's up and starting to collect acorns off the ground again. good grief. now she's cleaning the gutters. the gutters! i'm shaking my head from left to right. i can't help but smile. this is my wife, this woman, she can't stop moving. she's been an absolute pitbull advocating for me during a summer's worth of jumping through hospital health hoops, but if you ever met her in person you'd never guess how much of a beast this beauty really is.

she never rests.

she says it's the reason she stays sane. i say it's the reason i'm still alive.

Xo

•

Layton knew his short-term memory was starting to go because Candace had learned to ask simple questions while he was in the middle of a seizure or after he'd come out of one, and he could never answer them correctly. Sometimes, she'd give him a word to remember and he would only be able to recall the fuzzy outlines of the letters, or how many syllables it contained. But after an hour or so, he could feel the fog in his brain lifting, his world coming back into focus.

He was in and out of the hospital often these days—to have scans, to get the results of scans, to discuss the next course of treatment with his team of doctors. It no longer brought out the same anxiety in him that it once did. In fact, he sometimes made light of the situation—or at least tried to. He'd get Candace to take pictures of him trying on a stethoscope that had been foolishly left out before the doctor arrived in the room.

There was this routine Candace and Layton would do on Layton's worst days, when he felt an overwhelming sense he'd lost himself, that he'd been sucked down a drain.

"Where's Layton?" Candace would ask with concern.

"I don't know," he'd reply, defeated.

"Oh, he'll be back," she'd say reassuringly.

"Really?" he'd ask.

"Yeah, he's just buried in worry dirt," she'd say.

Buried in worry dirt. He liked that. It suggested sadness was temporary, something you could disappear into but then just as easily dig yourself out from.

thanksgiving dinner.

it always reminds me of the insanity that was the intensive natural cancer therapy i was on while we tried to keep my sorry ass alive by consuming the exact opposite of what the majority of us are enjoying this long weekend.

turkey and mother f*cking gravy, y'all.

it was a long twenty-two months, and the afternoon we

finally discovered that the therapy wasn't working was not a good day. i wish i could say i accepted it gracefully. i did not. i cried and laid on the ground in the backyard and pulled some hair out and punched a tree and kicked my shoes across the lawn. after nearly two years of countless hours, dollars and sanity that resulted in relatively stable scans it felt like getting punched in the stomach and kicked in the face simultaneously.

but if we've learned anything, this little clan of ours, it's that the way you react to shitty situations is the key to making it through tough times without losing your shit completely. for me, for now at least, sharing bits and pieces of our story has been therapeutic.

i can't make you feel what it's like to be a young, dumb, naive thirty-year-old sitting in the back of a walk-in clinic waiting to be handed what is essentially a death sentence any more than i can show you what it feels like to have a husband or father or child who's dying and knowing there is nothing you can do to stop it. i can only describe to you how i feel today. angry. at peace. scared. grateful. a giant, spiky, flowering heart-shaped bouquet of contradictions.

for better or worse there are days that just suck the good out of you. your spirit, your strength and your hope. and then there are days when the universe seems to rally around your cause when all prospects seem lost at that particular moment. this week contained one of those days. a day that started in tears and frustration and ended in optimism and thankfulness and maybe even a little irony considering the holiday we're currently celebrating this weekend.

so for now we lift our heads and our drumsticks high
and try our best to appreciate just how far we've come. and
maybe even how far we get to go.

happy thanksgiving gang.

save me some stuffing.

Xo

•

Sometimes, Candace felt like she couldn't shake Layton out of
his sullenness. His mind would often wander to what it might be
like to be the victim of a rape, a murder, a violent assault. To be
a kid growing up in a war zone without access to water. It wasn't
an exercise meant to make him feel good about his relative situation, but there were times when he liked to double down on
the darkness that so often consumed his thoughts. Push it to its
limits. Make the tunnel he was in a bit longer.

During the Gerson days, there was a goal everyone had
agreed to rally around, specific responsibilities each person
was assigned, and it had focused Candace in a way she was
now nostalgic for. She didn't miss the demands of that period,
but it had been a helpful distraction. Now she found herself
resenting Layton and then feeling guilty about it. His assigned
duties around the house were doing the dishes and sweeping.
She knew he wanted to do more, and there were days when he
was so physically spent she felt awful watching him: it was
clear the task took every last drop of his energy to complete.
But she was spent too. She'd been spent for years. She'd find
herself occasionally complaining to friends about it, how she

felt unappreciated, but then would stop short, wondering if her complaints sounded petty. She was the healthy one, the one whose whole life lay ahead of her. What was she whining about?

Like all parents, she'd heard about the terrible twos, but she'd had no idea Finn would be so difficult to parent when he was three. He was constantly testing her, and between that and seeing Layton in his worst physical shape, it was a high-stress time for Candace at the house. She felt drained caring for Finn and wondered what it might be like to have a healthy husband who was doing half the work.

Layton was at the house every night now, but Candace sometimes felt the same loneliness she felt during that long stretch when Layton slept over at his parents' years earlier. She didn't need to go out on dates with her husband—all she wanted was to cuddle up in bed and watch something mind-numbing on Netflix while Layton rested his legs on top of hers, as they'd done so many nights before. But by early fall, when Candace suggested watching something after dinner, Layton shut her down. It was a waste of time to fix his attention on some fictional universe when he didn't have much time left, he'd say. Other times, he'd be so sleepy after eating supper and washing dishes that he'd go upstairs and collapse in bed, leaving Candace awake and alone for a few hours. It had been months since they'd had sex and she wondered if it would ever happen again.

•

There weren't many options left for Layton now. Only one of his many brain tumours was operable, and his doctors didn't think removing it was worth the risk of damaging surrounding areas. They said there was little benefit to more radiation, and that at this point it would likely do more harm than good. Layton's medical team was controlling his symptoms with steroids, anti-seizure medications, and the drug he'd been taking for the last year.

But then they heard about a new drug, Keytruda, that seemed like it might help—or at least buy him more time. The problem was, it cost eleven thousand dollars per injection every three weeks and wasn't funded by the government. Layton's insurance provider wouldn't cover it either unless he took a different, cheaper drug first and proved that it didn't work for him. Layton's oncologist, meanwhile, didn't want him to take that cheaper drug because of the terrible side effects.

Candace found herself being completely distracted at work. She sent Layton an email every few hours, checking in: "You okay? Still alive?" Soon after the phone call with her mother about whether or not she should begin her compassionate care leave, Candace decided it was time. Now, in September, she'd been off for weeks with the goal of spending time with Layton, but they'd seen little of each other: Candace was on the phone every day, advocating for funding for the drug through Layton's insurance company or the government or the drug's manufacturer. She was also tied up with calls to ensure her pay was still coming through while she was on leave.

Layton finally got the funding for Keytruda from the pharmaceutical company in early October, after a full month of frantic phone calls from Candace and some patient advocates who had offered to help. The timing couldn't have been better, as he got the news right after a depressing morning appointment in which his doctor presented him with a few bleak options for the next steps. The process was going to begin the next day with an adjustment of his medications— and it was understood that this was the last hope for him. If this drug failed, they would wait and let nature run its course.

hey gang.

do you know what's kind of hard to talk about?

dying.

especially when you're not exactly sure when that's about to happen.

maybe in a month? maybe in six?

all we know today is this will most likely be our last option of treatment for my friends in the attic and i'm not going to take the risk and forget to say thank you for every bit of support you've all given us over the last few years. to me, my wife, my son and my family. i owe you gang, don't you forget that.

admittedly, it's a pretty strange feeling, still having the ability to say goodbye, regardless of when exactly that may happen. it's a gift, and it's definitely one i don't want to waste. i just need to cover my bases today and remind you all as a collective how much love i've felt throughout this process of sharing and i promise to do my best to remember your words of encouragement, support, love and good vibes when things start declining,

whether that's physically or mentally or both at the same
time.

   until then, you know who you are and you know how
much love i've got for you and that's all we'll say about that
today before i allow myself to get too emotional, dammit.

   cool? cool. big hugs my friends. let's keep on moving.

   onward & upward.

   we're not done yet.

   Xo

·

At the end of the month, Layton completed his final 5K race.
Though his pace was lagging, Layton still liked to keep track
of his time. He was crushed by how slow he was now, but
he reminded himself of what he'd been saying all year since he
started training: *I'm not dead if I'm running.*

   The seizures Layton was having now were different from
before. They weren't full-body convulsions, but instead a wave
of nausea and a scramble of memories that briefly flashed in his
brain like a faulty slide projector. He'd be sitting in his bed and
then feel the rush of one come on—it was like the sensation of
dreaming, but he knew he was awake. The dreams were usually
about very specific things that happened in the past, but he
rarely remembered much once he snapped out of it—like a
dream might fade completely from memory between waking
up and brushing one's teeth. The seizures were getting less
intense but more frequent—they'd become daily occurrences.
When he was on his own, he knew he'd had a seizure if he

couldn't remember what happened earlier in the day because the seizures had a way of permanently wiping out the hours that preceded them. But Layton figured this wasn't just the tumours but also his lack of sleep—that being hard to find now with Finn waking up early and also the steroids taking their toll. These days it was the norm that by evening he couldn't account for what had happened in the morning. It could have been due to the tumours, or radiation, or a combination of the two. Sometimes, he'd find posts he'd put on Facebook and have no recollection of writing them, or of how long the process took.

One of Layton's primary fears now was not finishing all his projects for Finn before he died, including Eve's suggestion of a collection of letters that Finn was to be given at various milestones—starting elementary school/junior high/ high school/university, losing his virginity, his first breakup, getting his driver's licence, having a fight with Candace, marriage, kids, Candace's death.

One day, he declared the Finn Box finished—if only because his faculties were failing too much now for him to make meaningful changes to it. He thought back to what Eve had written to him about what her husband had left behind for his sons when he died: "I know that whatever you leave will never seem to you to be enough: at the same time these gifts will go farther than you think."

He had a habit of writing notes for Candace to read after his death in the clean, minimalist style he favoured. Black felt-tip pen. Everything in lowercase. Lettering consistent, like a bespoke typeface. And then sealed in his signature kraft paper envelopes. After giving his parents a stack of these letters, he asked for them back, worried he might have repeated the same sentiments in some. "I know I put some poems and stuff in there. I don't know if they're all right," he confessed to them sheepishly. He'd also entrusted his parents with a pair of USB drives and asked for those back, too, wanting to know what was on them. He contemplated making a checklist of all the things he wanted to leave behind, but even that required more brain power than he had these days.

He also had recurring daily fears about what it would feel like to die. When he had several consecutive days of feeling crummy, he wondered, like he had during his Gerson days, if this was the marker of the final stretch. Was he fading? Would the next seizure leave him permanently changed—unable to feel one side of his body? He wanted a first-person account to read that guided him through each painful or terrifying or peaceful second of the experience, though he also knew he was too scared to engage with something like that. How was he going to feel just before he died? Would he know he was dying in those final moments? Or would it be like he was living one second and—*surprise!*—not the next?

But more than that, he so desperately wanted to look into the future and see what Finn would be like as a teenager. What shape Candace's life would take after he was gone. Would she be happy? Would she change careers? Would she find someone else to love the way she had loved him?

While Layton was obsessed with what the future would look like, parts of Candace yearned to jump back a decade, to experience that simpler existence for a little while. Her favourite moments of the day were in the mornings now: she liked cooking something, even eggs, and bringing them up to Layton's room to eat while she sat on the bed beside him. In that space of half an hour in the morning, the chaos of the day hadn't yet set in. She wasn't a mom yet, or an employee. It was just her and Layton, like when she was twenty-one or twenty-five or thirty.

During these breakfasts, Layton tried to summon what little strength he had to be present for Candace. The truth was, he could barely get any sleep these days no matter how much time he spent in bed summoning slumber. He was like a phone that had been plugged in overnight but whose charger had been knocked out of the outlet.

By mid-November, during one of Layton's appointments, Candace asked the doctor how long she thought Layton had left. Three months? Six months? The doctor said three months, maybe one month, maybe less. And though Layton stood out in the hallway, still preferring to be blissfully ignorant, it was clear to her that he knew.

The wit that characterized all his correspondence had disappeared. His notes were short. Sometimes, he'd reply to the same email twice, but with different responses. He got the impression from Candace that his oncologist was convinced he was on his way out, and it made him angry to know that the team that was supposed to save him seemed to have thrown in the towel. He occasionally ended emails to me saying he missed me, but I noticed a shift in his signoffs that signalled he understood he had only weeks left. In early December, he wrote:

my present moment is off but i'll be back i hope soon enough, my friend. i miss you today and i'll miss you forever from here on out.

I read it again and again and again, more than anything else he'd sent me. The phrase "i'll miss you forever" came to me in the shower, it interrupted the podcasts I listened to on my commute to work, it ran through my brain after I turned off the bedroom light and got under my duvet. His thinking had been getting cloudier in such a measurable way, but everything about that message suggested mental clarity, an awareness of exactly what was happening to him. Two weeks later, he sent me an email where I could tell he was struggling with the simple tasks of thinking and typing.

> *hi bud.*
> *i'm so sorry it's just most likely i've got pretty close to what i've got these days lately again returning again. i'll do my best to get some. thank you for the patience my friend.*

The next day, he reread what he wrote and knew it didn't express what he wanted to say, but he also didn't have the ability to communicate that to me, so he asked Candace to follow up.

> *hey d,*
> *c here. l just re-read his last response to you and realized it doesn't make any sense. :(good days and bad as you know, he's still a bit off. thanks for checking in . . . love from Halifax . . . xo*

six

One morning in December, Irma received a text from her daughter, who said she was worried about Layton. Candace didn't ask Irma to come over, but Irma knew that's what she wanted, so she left her work behind and headed to the house. Candace and Irma were sitting downstairs together when they heard a loud crash and raced upstairs: Layton had fallen from bed and was having a seizure. It didn't look like what Irma expected: he was sitting on the floor but wasn't conscious. They tried speaking to him, asking what happened, if he was okay, but he couldn't respond. It was like he didn't register that they were there. They tried to help him get back into bed, but it was like moving a sandbag: his motor skills were gone, he was heavy and immobile. They directed him to lift this particular limb or that one, but he couldn't. Candace, ever the grounded, organized one, called an ambulance and calmly explained what had happened, as though this were the thousandth time she'd dialled 911. Even in the midst of this chaos, Irma marvelled at her daughter's calm demeanour, remembering how Candace had always been like this. She was the child who made lists, who was never needlessly emotional. Dealing with Layton's illness for so many years had only sharpened this ability to stay so composed in times of crisis.

At the hospital, doctors assessed Layton and gave Candace the news she had been dreading for a long time: this last seizure had been a particularly bad one and had greatly impacted his cognitive function. He maybe had only a few days left. Layton didn't need to hear this from doctors—he could feel it himself.

When his mother arrived at the hospital, Layton was as vulnerable as he'd ever been with her. "That was a great big seizure I had," he told her, with a trace of childlike wonder. "I could have died there and it would've been okay."

He caught Willie's eyes. "Mom, I'm dying."

Layton was admitted to the palliative care ward that day, and it was understood this was where he would die. The space wasn't private: there was a shared entryway, shared bathroom, and an area with cubbies for each patient. All that separated Layton from the woman in the next bed was a curtain. She was dying too, and it seemed to be a more painful experience: she had an obstructed bowel and was up all night, very agitated, with staff visiting hourly, trying to get her to use the commode. People who were with her made loud phone calls at all hours. Willie contemplated saying something to the woman's son, who was the loudest of the bunch, but then thought, *His mother is dying. This isn't my place.*

It was such a different experience from when Willie's father had been in palliative care at another hospital. The environment was soothing and quiet—there wasn't the constant soundtrack of the radio, which in Layton's ward blared Top 40 or obnoxious AM jockeys at all times (Willie later learned from a nurse that this was to give a sense of company to patients who didn't have constant visitors). On that first night, Willie stayed in the lounge and Candace lay in bed beside Layton, but there was no rest for anyone.

Candace and Layton had spoken before about where he would die, and Layton always said his preference was to do it at home but that ultimately it was Candace's choice. She agreed that this was the best scenario but accepted that if he needed special equipment in the end that they didn't have at home, they'd have to do it at the hospital.

After only one day, Candace and Willie agreed they needed to find a way to get Layton back to the house. It was two days before Christmas and they begged doctors to allow it, to get the equipment home so Layton could live out his last few days in peace. The palliative team put a rush on getting an occupational therapist, visiting nurses, and a home care team to see Layton that very day, a Friday, so they could release him before the hospital switched to holiday hours.

Even with the approvals, Layton was hesitant. "I don't want to ruin the house for you," he told Candace. "If dying here would ruin the house for you, let's not do it."

·

When Layton returned home from the hospital, several medical devices came with him: a walker, a tub transfer, a raised toilet seat, none of which he wanted to use. Watching him look at all of it was heart-wrenching for Willie. For years, Layton would always jokingly begin sentences with, "When I'm shitting myself . . . ," as though that was the true marker of decrepitude, of a life no longer worth living. He was nearly at that stage now. Willie had been so used to caring for him but knew now that the last thing he wanted was to be looked after by his mother. If he needed anything, he wanted it to come from Candace or the nurse on duty. It crushed her.

There was a commode kept in Layton's room so that on his weaker days he wouldn't need to walk to the bathroom, but he refused to use that, too. If he had to crawl to get to the toilet, so be it. Sometimes, Phil would wait outside the bathroom door when Layton was inside, listening for signs of distress, knowing his son would never call out if he needed help or had a fall.

At first, Layton could get in and out of bed on his own, but that eventually became a struggle, so they moved a hospital bed into his room. The queen-sized bed he and Candace had slept on was now pushed against the wall under the window. The hospital bed was aligned with the door so Layton could look down the hallway and into Finn's room while he was lying down. He spent all his time in his room and the bathroom, unable to come down the stairs. Willie, having seen her son nearly every day for the previous three years, was quick to notice the subtle changes in Layton, the small difficulties he was having.

It had become a tradition that the family spent Christmas Eve at Layton and Candace's, dining on something fun and decidedly unfestive, like fish tacos, and this year, even though Layton was far too weak and exhausted to host, they maintained the tradition. He didn't greet guests when they arrived— he was up in bed, too wiped even to shift position—but Phil came up to chat and keep him company before returning to the family, who were on the main floor. Suddenly, there was stirring upstairs and then a few minutes later Layton's thin frame appeared at the top of the stairs, slowly descending each step on his butt, using his hands to stabilize himself. He made his way to the living room in a drawn-out shuffle and sighed, "I'll try to do this."

"This" was something he'd been looking forward to for months: reading "'Twas the Night Before Christmas" to his son on what he knew to be his last Christmas. Layton sat on the sofa with the book open, his soft voice drowned out by all the activity around him. Instead of obediently perching in his father's lap, Finn raced around the living room with a dish full of acorns, a child who couldn't possibly understand the gravity of the situation. Daddy read to him every night and always would—why did he have to sit silently now?

The next day, Layton was more exhausted than usual—the price of heading downstairs the previous day to read to Finn—but was determined to celebrate one last Christmas at Willie and Phil's. They reassured him that nobody expected him to attend, that he should stay home and rest, but Layton was adamant. "I don't want to fuck up Christmas for everybody," he said.

By the time he reached his parents' place, he'd expended all his energy for the day, and with one person standing in front of him and one behind him, Layton climbed up the stairs and collapsed on the bed in his parents' guest room—the same one he'd spent all those nights on in the thick of Gerson. In these last few weeks, even if he did have the stamina to join the others, he was often quiet and withdrawn, worried about how social interactions, even with family, would go now that his memory was failing him. Conversations didn't have their same flow. His wit was gone, as though a tumour had now spread to the part of his brain responsible for humour. He'd say something, and if there was a pause before the person he was speaking to responded, a look of panic would register on his face. "Did I tell you that already?" he'd ask, embarrassed.

A few weeks earlier, he'd told Irma he had something he wanted her to buy for Candace for Christmas on his behalf. But after that sentence was uttered, he couldn't figure out the one that followed. What was the thing he wanted Irma to buy? He never did remember, but ended up finding another gift for Candace, or at least he thought he did. The problem was, he couldn't remember where he'd put it. He argued with Candace about it one day, taking his temper out on her when really he hated himself and his brain for failing him so spectacularly. They were like an elderly couple bickering: one still clear-headed, the other battling dementia.

While Layton rested on Christmas Day, Matt's kids, Trevor and Mitchell, were in the next room with Finn, watching *A Charlie Brown Christmas*. At one point, Trevor wandered into the room where Layton was sleeping, with Willie fast on his tail. "What's Uncle Layton doing in my bed?" he asked. On the days when Willie and Phil babysat Trevor, this was the room where he napped.

"He's resting, honey, he's not feeling very well," Willie explained.

Layton stirred awake. His eyelids were at half-mast and he flashed his nephew a small smile. "Hey buddy," he whispered.

Before the meal was served, a few people went upstairs again to help Layton out of bed and down the stairs for dinner. Willie had cooked all his favourites: roasted turkey with stuffing made from chicken sausage, bread crumbs, celery, and apples. She'd prepared chicken, too, for Finn and Candace, alongside roasted vegetables and gravy. Layton was exhausted, in pain, and having a tough time even forming words. He could only pick at his food.

On New Year's Eve, everyone knew Layton wouldn't be able to stay up until midnight, so Finn climbed into bed with his father and they did an early countdown in the middle of the day, ringing in the new year while it was still light out.

•

For years, Willie silently cringed watching her adult sons interact. After Matt visited the house, Layton would confess to his mother that it was painful to see his brother—he often felt more comfortable around Matt's wife. The times when Matt went to see Layton in the hospital, he was always so anxious. Was he supposed to go in and get real and serious and ask Layton how he was doing? To talk to him about treatment? Be . . . heavy? Or was he supposed to keep things light and breezy? What did other people talk to Layton about, anyway? How did they navigate this? It felt easier to speak to his mom in those situations, and he came to rely on her presence. He thought of it like a group conversation, where Layton could jump in whenever he wanted. But he didn't. It was always Matt and Willie talking in the room as if Layton wasn't even there. Matt knew he wasn't being the best brother he could be, but he didn't know what else to do at the time.

After a friend recommended it, Matt made an appointment to see a grief counsellor. Maybe this would give him a chance to sort out his feelings about his brother's illness, about the impending loss, the friend said. Matt, however, saw this more as an opportunity to figure out why he was unhappy—this was simply long-overdue therapy. He realized that every time he went to see his brother, he felt an overwhelming urge to cut the small talk and unload on Layton about his own unhappiness. But something always stopped him. How could he do this now, after being so distant with Layton, when Layton was so clearly close to death? It seemed so inappropriate to simply say, "This is a thing I'm going through."

He'd spent the seven years of his brother's illness in the first of the Kübler-Ross stages: denial. Was it the fog of parenthood? Some mild version of a mid-life crisis? The odd time he went to see Layton, he seemed lucid and pain-free, so despite the Stage IV diagnosis, the situation never seemed truly dire to Matt.

Even though Layton was the one who was going to die and he was the one who was going to live, Matt felt some sense of that familiar brotherly envy he'd had for Layton so much of his life: here was his brother, even in this end stage, with so much clarity. He was the guy who'd figured out how to make the most of the little time he still had left. It was impressive, and mildly annoying.

When winter came, Matt started emailing Layton more, but everything was surface level. He'd send him goofy things he saw online, or photos he took that he was proud of. Then there were the half-hearted attempts to make plans. "I'm doing a show at this place tonight" or "Come see me at this open mic." After a series of vague invitations like this, Layton responded very frankly to him, confessing that the times they had gotten together had been awkward. Though Layton tried to soften his message by saying the meds he was on made him less fun to spend time with, Matt accepted a lot of the blame for what their relationship had become.

But then there was a more direct invitation, almost a challenge, from Layton: "Look, your brother's on his way out and if there's anything you want to say to me, this is probably a good time to do it." He listed off the things he appreciated and respected about Matt and then told him, "If there's anything you want, I need you to do the work."

Matt was so grateful for that message. He replied, telling Layton how much he meant to him, how proud he was of his accomplishments in photography and admitted that, in his mind, he'd always thought of Layton as the cooler Reid brother.

They'd had a few lunch dates over the years since Layton had moved back to Halifax—Matt would pick him up and they'd drive to a diner. Ahead of Christmas or Mother's Day, they'd make a trip to Walmart and take goofy pictures together in the portrait studio to present to Willie as a gift—giving the illusion, at least in those cheesy 8x10s, that they were the sort of brothers who had an intimate, inside-joke-filled relationship.

When visiting in January, Matt told Layton they should go to Walmart again and do a long session with several outfit changes to bank them for future years. It was a fantasy and they both knew it—Layton couldn't even leave his room now, let alone the house. But he smiled and said, "Yeah, sounds good."

In trying to make sense of his strained relationship with his brother, Matt read up on the subject. He took some comfort in learning that adult male friendships are more challenging to maintain than female ones, especially if sports aren't involved. The way he and Layton had difficulty relating was normal, he told himself. Layton had his friends he ran with or played basketball with, but Matt wasn't interested in those things, so how was he supposed to bond with his athletic brother? I could never figure out why Layton and Matt were the way they were with each other. And because they couldn't either, there was little hope of fixing anything.

It was Matt's son Trevor's birthday around this time, and Matt took what he thought was a beautiful picture of Finn at the party. He emailed it to Layton, eager for his approval, but the attachment didn't go through. Layton replied, saying, "Thanks but I can't see it" and that was the last email Matt received from him. More than wanting to be loved by Layton, Matt longed to impress him.

•

It was a weekend in mid-January when it became clear to Candace that Layton as she knew him was long gone. Getting up to use the bathroom or even the commode in his room was difficult for him. Any task that required multiple steps became too confusing. Candace would patiently walk Layton through the process, one that for three and a half decades had been built into his muscle memory but that was now too complicated without a coach. She'd repeat herself again and again, but it was clear that wires were getting crossed.

"Sit up," she'd tell Layton. "Okay," he'd say, but would stay in the same position. "Sit up," she'd encourage him again. "Okay," he'd repeat, immobile.

One day, when Willie was down in the kitchen washing dishes, a nurse, who was with Layton in his room, asked her if she had any food she could offer him. Willie brought up a bowl of chicken soup a few minutes later and her heart ached as Layton struggled to consume it with a spoon. After watching him for several painful seconds, she could no longer fight the instinct that she was a mother and this was her little boy and she offered to feed him. He refused. He wasn't able to get down much of the soup, swallowing had become so difficult, but he was trying desperately to maintain whatever kind of control he could over his life.

There was a baby monitor in Finn's room, and now it felt necessary to get a second monitor to keep an eye on Layton. Sometimes, it didn't seem like he realized he was in a hospital bed, like he even knew where he was. One night, Candace was downstairs and she heard rustling coming from the second floor. She looked at both baby monitors, and in Layton's, she could see he was moving around in a state of confusion. It seemed he wanted to go to the bathroom, but after sitting up at the edge of his hospital bed, he'd yet again forgotten what the next steps were. Candace climbed the stairs and, upon reaching her husband's bedside, saw a look of defeat on his face, one she'd not seen before. She could tell he was done. Done with everything.

"I just want to go home," Layton said softly. The line was familiar to Candace—she remembered reading about other terminal patients saying this in their final days.

"What do you mean? What's home to you?" she asked.

"Wherever you are," he whispered.

Days earlier, Candace had been sure he no longer recognized her—he'd sometimes mix up Candace and Irma, and once, in a state of disorientation, seemed to lean in for a kiss when his mother-in-law was at his bedside. But here was a brief moment of lucidity. It was what Candace needed. "I know, this is our home," she said to him, her voice cracking.

The next morning Finn bounded into Layton's room, bringing surplus energy as if to compensate for how drained his father was. The two sat together with matching breakfasts: multi-grain bagels with organic smooth peanut butter (Layton did not abide by the crunchy kind) topped with slices of perfectly ripe bananas (Finn did not abide by the too-sweet kind) and glasses of orange juice.

At lunchtime, Candace tried to give Layton his pills and, in a daze, he rolled them from his tongue to his molars and bit down on them. "No, no, no, no, don't chew that!" Candace scolded. He could hear her but wasn't computing what she was saying. She locked eyes with him and explained, "I'm going to put my fingers in your mouth. But don't bite my fingers, okay?" And she carefully removed the pills.

Fearing this might happen again, she called the palliative care team and they changed some of his medications to their injectable form. That afternoon, Layton closed his eyes. At first, Candace thought he might be asleep, but he was unresponsive. A nurse explained he might not wake up. He might be like this for another week or two. And he might start to have apneas, periods when he would stop breathing. The apneas would last longer as he inched towards death, which already seemed so close. A nurse was in the room the first time Layton had one. *Is he going to die while she's here?* Candace wondered, watching his face and chest intently, hoping he'd inhale again. He did, and before he could even exhale, Candace was in tears. The nurse hugged her, steadying her body as it shook with sobs.

After four years of holding it together, Candace was finally allowing herself to lose her composure in front of other people. She cried messily as her mother sat beside her, as nurses came to record Layton's vitals, as Willie and Phil stood by their son's bedside, as a home-care worker put fresh clothes on Layton's now nearly motionless body. As the woman lifted Layton's long legs and wriggled his pants off, he moaned a few times, but to Candace, this was an involuntary sound coming from a body whose spirit had already left it.

Candace didn't sleep much for the next few days. She was in the same room as Layton and she'd slow her own breathing at night, keeping an ear out for the periods when Layton's inhalations and exhalations ceased, as though she could calculate when he'd die by studying the gaps between apneas—like she'd done with her contractions when she was in labour. The sounds Layton made as he struggled to breathe offered no comfort. Each breath was sharp, slow, and ragged—as though the mere act of inhaling was taxing his body. Eventually, it became so hard to listen to that she moved downstairs to sleep on the couch and brought the baby monitors with her.

Finn kissed his father goodnight every evening before Candace put him to bed, and was so accustomed to carrying on with Layton that the first night when he saw him sleeping, he thought his father was playing around. But now Layton was in a permanent state of slumber. Finn crept up to his bed and tried to pry his father's eyelids open with his fingers, to kiss him on the cheek.

"Daddy's eyes can't open," Candace told him. "He's asleep now and he's not going to wake up. You can still hear him breathing and if you talk to him, he can hear you."

Finn was always told, "Daddy's going to the doctor," to explain his father's many trips to the hospital. He got used to the long stretches when Layton would be confined to his room, only descending for dinner, and sometimes he'd say, "Daddy's going to get better and then he can play with me." Candace would have to set him straight again and again: "No, honey, daddy's not going to get better." It finally seemed time for Candace to give her son the whole truth. A palliative nurse had counselled her to be honest, to use simple, straightforward language, not euphemism. "Kids can process more than we give them credit for," she said.

That night, Candace sat with her son. "Daddy has cancer and he's not going to get better. The doctors tried to make him better, but they couldn't make him better," she said. She held him tightly as he cried, absorbing this information with his young brain.

Knowing how difficult the relationship between her sons could be, Willie never forced Matt to see Layton, but this was the end, and Willie knew she'd have to nudge her eldest son to make a move. "I can't say it's okay for you to come. It has to be Candace," she told him.

Candace welcomed Matt, and began texting him directly, encouraging him to stop by the house. These visits were a bit easier since Matt didn't have to worry about whether he was entertaining Layton or saying the right thing. He didn't need his mother as a buffer. He'd ramble about issues going on with a particular work project he had. He wasn't sure if his brother was asleep or processing the things he was saying. One day, when he was leaving, Matt leaned in to give Layton a quick hug and kiss on the cheek, and when his lips made contact with his brother's skin, Layton's eyes fluttered open briefly. Could Layton see him? Was he happy he'd come? Or if he'd had control of his body, would he have pulled away from the kiss?

After visiting three days in a row, Matt was out on a skating rink one day and received a text from his mother suggesting he was maybe stopping by Layton's house too much. "Candace would probably like to have some time," she told him.

Willie and Phil made brief visits every afternoon, and it was at this point that Willie knew it was her cue to tell Layton the last things she wanted to tell him. She'd heard "the death rattle" in both her parents before they passed and figured her son was on the precipice.

Jenn Grant, a singer-songwriter from Halifax, was an old school friend of Candace's, and Layton had met her many years later when both worked as cater waiters. Since then, the two had intermittently been in touch, but she'd had a profound effect on Layton: her 2014 album, *Compostela*, had become the soundtrack to Layton's life. It was based on a trip Jenn took to Spain when she was processing her mother's death, and it dealt so plainly and vulnerably with grief and memory that it became a salve to Layton, a reassurance that Finn and Candace's lives would go on after he was gone but that he'd still be connected to them. He often thought about the lyrics from his favourite track, "Barcelona": *Time will take us but cannot break us, time will keep us together.* He listened to a steady soundtrack of sad songs after they found the brain tumours, finding them cathartic. Candace called it "slit your wrist music" but Layton liked leaning into sadness—pushing the bruise and then, before the pain had a chance to fade, pushing it again.

On Wednesday afternoon, when Willie and Phil went to visit him, Phil put on *Compostela*, hoping it might wake something up in his son, or at the very least soothe him. Phil had heard the album for the first time only a few days earlier at home. "No one's gonna love you, quite like I doooo-ooooo," Jenn sang to a motionless Layton, and Willie and Phil told their son not to worry about Candace and Finn.

Willie never told Layton she hoped his death would come quickly, but she believed he felt it—that his mother wanted him to be rescued from the pain swiftly. She was convinced he wanted to get through Christmas for Candace, but now that he had, there was nothing left in him.

One nurse warned Candace that because Layton was no longer on his oral medications, it was likely his seizures would return. She showed Candace the stash of pre-measured medications she'd brought and taught her how to connect a syringe to an intravenous line in Layton's arm so she could inject them into Layton's bloodstream if he started to have a seizure. There was a different set of instructions for administering morphine if he was in pain.

But Layton couldn't talk, hadn't opened his eyes. How was she supposed to know when to do what?

"You'll know," the nurse told her. "Trust your gut."

And so Candace erred on the side of administering painkillers whenever she had the slightest inkling her husband was uncomfortable. If he'd moan, she'd give him morphine. If he seemed a bit restless, she'd give him morphine. She knew he couldn't overdose on the amount she was giving him, and she'd rather give him too much than too little. After this long journey, this was the last way she could help him. Days passed like this, and Candace often felt detached. Layton seemed like a body in the room.

Irma began spending nights at the house, leaving for her own home in the morning to shower and change, and then returning later in the day. She spent long hours sitting beside Layton in his room as he lay motionless. Could he hear what was going on around him? Was he replying in his head? Irma assumed he was conscious of the world around him, and she talked to him as though he was awake, updating him about how work was going for her, about a funny thing Finn said the previous evening, the general mundanities of life. But there were challenges in this small talk. How could she comment on the beautiful snowfall outside when Layton couldn't look out the window? The one-way conversation would always turn to the same point, which she felt she couldn't tell him enough: that Candace and Finn would be taken care of.

Layton's lips were dry and cracked from his breathing through them. One day, when Candace tried to moisten them with water, Layton's jaw tightened. Without oxygen entering his body, his skin took on a blue cast—it seemed like he was asphyxiating. *Is he dying?* Candace wondered. *Is this happening right now?* She grabbed one of his hands and Irma took the other. "It's okay," they repeated to him gently. But then the moment passed and blood journeyed through his veins back to his cheeks, returning them to their normal colour. His jaw relaxed. He was breathing again. Candace realized then he'd had a seizure—this is what it looked like in the state he was in. *Layton really does have nine lives*, she thought.

Later that evening, Candace was downstairs talking with a friend who'd dropped by while Irma was upstairs with Layton when the same thing happened: Layton's jaw clenched and his eyelids fluttered. His body shook slightly and he breathed sharply through his nose, like a bull. Irma walked to the top of the stairs and called down for Candace. Candace shooed the friend out and raced to Layton's room. She tried not to panic and fumbled around trying to find the syringe, made sure the dosage was correct, and injected it. In a few seconds, after the medication had entered his bloodstream, Layton relaxed. Candace instantly felt regret that she hadn't given him the injection earlier in the day, when he was having his first seizure. Her final job, her promise to him, was to take away his suffering. He seemed stable now, but she knew that two seizures in one day meant something significant was happening in his brain.

After that seizure, Irma was convinced Layton would die within a day. Even after he came to, his breathing was more laboured than ever. He made a gurgling noise when he inhaled, and his chest would rise like a tent. Each breath was slow but sharp. Though his body was only devoted to this one task, even that seemed too much for him.

Around 9 p.m., Layton stopped breathing. Irma was in the room with him, and when Candace came to join her, they both looked at each other and counted the seconds in their heads. *This was probably an apnea*, they thought, and waited five minutes, assuming he'd begin breathing again. He didn't. They waited five more minutes. Should Candace call Layton's parents? But what if he started breathing again? More minutes passed. Finally, it felt real.

Candace thought back to the injection she'd given him earlier. Did she relax him too much? Was that what pushed him over the edge? What was the point dwelling on any of that now, though? There were things to do.

At 9:30, she called Willie and Phil. Willie was in bed, Phil was doing dishes in the kitchen.

"I'm so sorry, he's gone," she told Willie as soon as she picked up, her voice ragged.

Willie had known for a long time this moment was coming. She wasn't going to break down on the phone. "Would it be okay if we come?" she asked.

"Oh yeah, yeah of course," Candace said.

Willie and Phil were so used to driving from their house, in the west end of the city, to their son's, a few kilometres south, that they could have made the trip with their eyes closed, especially at this time of night when the dark streets were so empty. Those few minutes in the car offered a release: a time, in silence, for each to process what had happened.

After the phone call, Candace and Irma sat in Layton's room and took turns crying. Candace wanted to cuddle her husband, but the hospital bed was too small for her to climb into, so she draped herself over its edge and hugged Layton, sobbing into his hoodie.

Irma's body crumpled beside her. "I'm supposed to be comforting you, but I can't," she told her daughter.

When Willie and Phil arrived at the house and walked up into their son's room, they were surprised by the surreal silence. For days, there was a steady soundtrack of Layton's laboured breathing, but now it was pin-drop quiet. Layton had a look of absolute serenity on his face. In the last few days, it sometimes seemed like his body was in a rictus, going through the dying process. Now, in death, his muscles had finally relaxed. Willie had an instinct to take a picture of her son's peaceful slumber but held back. *No, that wouldn't be appropriate*, she thought.

She and Phil spent twenty minutes in the room with Layton, in silence. Then Willie went back downstairs and sent a text message to Matt. "Hi honey, your brother's gone," she wrote. A reply came immediately, not from Matt but from one of Willie's dearest friends, to whom she'd mistakenly sent the text. After comforting her friend and setting her straight, Willie then sent the message to her son, the living one, about her other son, the dead one.

Then everyone gathered in the living room, which was illuminated by the erratic bursts of orange flame from the wood stove. They stared into the fire for a long time in silence. Candace had planned to spend the night downstairs with her mom as usual, but it didn't feel right. "I'm going to sleep upstairs," she told Irma. Candace climbed into the bed she'd shared for so many years with her husband as he lay a few feet away. This felt right. There was a strange energy in the air, like she could feel he was still there. Layton was gone, but he also wasn't gone yet.

As Candace pulled up the covers and stretched out on the mattress, she felt a reassuring weight on the right side of her body, like Layton was lying in bed with her in his familiar position: one leg resting on top of hers. She opened her eyes in the darkness and quietly said, "I can feel that you're here" and soon fell asleep. But in the morning, when she woke up, the feeling was gone. She walked over to Layton's bed and he didn't look like himself anymore—the colour had left his face, his body had gone cold and stiff. This made things easier in a way. *It's just a body now*, she thought. *There's no soul there.* She closed the door and walked into Finn's room. She'd heard him fussing all night. He'd woken up a few times and moaned. He sat up with a start when Candace opened the door.

"Mummy, there was a blue shadow walking towards the bed, but when you opened the door it went away!" he exclaimed. "It had really long legs, like a giraffe."

Candace was worried Finn would want to go in to see his dad before he went to daycare, like he so often did, but this morning it didn't come up. She was relieved.

Willie, meanwhile, was at home, about to start washing a pile of dishes in the sink. Before turning on the faucet, she looked up at the window and saw a large splatter of bird excrement and shook her head. But then it jumped out at her: the splatter was in the shape of a feather, like a painting some particularly rude but artistic pigeon had left behind.

She called Phil over to look. After Willie's mother had died, she started seeing feathers everywhere—a sign, she believed. A wave, a wink, a nudge. Layton knew about that and whenever he came across a feather, he'd give it to her. A real feather was Willie's mother but this bird shit one—this had to be Layton, right?

There you are with your bad self, making a mockery of the feather stuff! Willie thought, scolding her son in her mind but unable to resist smiling. She told Phil he was not allowed to clean it up. The snow or rain would take care of it one day, but for now she liked having it there.

That morning I woke up at six o'clock, turned off my phone's alarm, and saw an email from Candace telling me Layton had died. It had been a week since he and I had emailed, and I had gone to bed the previous three nights feeling something was wrong. I put my phone away and lay on my back, letting the news cover me like a heavy blanket. I cried silently, staring at the ceiling. My husband asked what had happened and I told him, but my own voice sounded strange to me, like I was underwater. I had never been this prepared for a death in my life, and still it took me by surprise. Layton had been to the brink and back so many times that it was too easy to picture myself knocking on his kitchen door again, or having him photograph a future child of mine. This felt like a long-distance breakup in its abstraction: I was intellectually aware of a profound loss, but nothing in my day-to-day felt immediately changed.

Back at the house, Candace made the call to the funeral home to inform them Layton had died, and when they arrived with the coroner, she left her mom to show them to his room and carry his body downstairs. She sat in the living room, not wanting to see her husband, now a corpse, leaving their home for the last time. Later, when she went up to his room, it was nice to see that the sheets had been stripped from the bed and taken with Layton. Somehow the missing linens made the bed just a medical apparatus again—one that could be removed easily. A thing that was no longer connected to Layton. The funeral home had asked what Layton wanted to be cremated in, and it made sense to go with what had been his second skin for so much of the last few years of his life: jeans, a white tee, a grey hoodie, and his slippers.

Since she'd learned that someone would have to go to the funeral home to identify Layton's body to ensure it was him, not someone else, who was cremated, Candace had dreaded that task and was relieved when Willie and Phil offered to do it. Their appointment was at 3:15 p.m., and she was startled when her phone lit up at 3:16 with a notification from Facebook that told her Layton Reid had posted that he was with her at that very minute. A few minutes later, she got another notification that he'd tagged her in a photograph of Finn playing with a pile of leaves. Layton hadn't logged into Facebook in weeks. He hadn't been awake in days. Hadn't been alive in hours. How could this be? She wanted to Google it, to see if this was some common glitch, but decided against it. Maybe there was a rational explanation, but she didn't want to know it. It was nice to think that in that moment when his body was about to turn to ash, he was reaching out to her one last time.

.

Layton had been stressed for months about his own memorial service. He didn't want any kind of religious component to it. He didn't want it in a stuffy, formal funeral home that felt like a church. He didn't want it in some cavernous venue that felt cold and empty, but he didn't want people to be standing outside the room because the space was too small, either.

"Layton, you just need to trust me," Candace had told him again and again.

Layton had insisted a life-sized cardboard cut-out of himself be present for the memorial, and the family postponed the service by a few days because there was a delay at the printer. The cut-out featured a very Layton-y photo of Layton, in which he was in frayed jeans, a white tee and raggedy toque, holding tiny, bundled-up infant Finn.

They were calling it a celebration of life, but still, this was a memorial service in a funeral home (which ended up being the most appropriate venue for such a gathering) so there was only so much Candace and Willie could do to fulfill Layton's wishes. When Willie arrived at the funeral home the day before the service, she pointed out some of the religious statues in the room to the staff. "Jesus has to go," she told them. Layton might have wanted a few hanging ferns and maybe a massive monstera decorating the space, but instead there were the typical stuffy bouquets of red and white roses, orange lilies, and few tall gladioli. He would've nixed flags on display at the front of the room—the Canadian, Nova Scotian, and Union Jack—but they were part of the permanent decor. The programs were printed on paper Layton never would've approved of in a font he would've mocked. He would've hated the carpet.

Candace briefly flirted with the idea of becoming a funeral director after organizing Layton's service. It felt like there was nothing in the packages and trimmings that were offered that suited a person younger than seventy-five. She was given a stack of thank-you cards to distribute to those who attended and knew she wouldn't send a single one: they were formal and stuffy and too serious, suited to a senior with a prized perennial garden, not her minimalist thirty-something husband.

The evening before the service, Candace brought Finn to the funeral home. She'd decided he wasn't old enough to attend the memorial, so they arranged for a private service just for him. Studying the cardboard cut-out, Finn recognized his father right away, and then, with much excitement, himself. "Baby Finnie!" he said, pointing.

Candace knew he understood Layton was gone. When she went to pick him up at daycare the day after Layton's death, one of the staff told her Finn had said, "My daddy's dead and now he's in a box" very matter-of-factly, as though he was stating he was wearing red shoes, or needed to go to the bathroom.

On the morning of the service, I arrived early, at the same time as some of Layton's silver-haired elementary school teachers. People streamed into the big, beige room in pairs or small clusters as Bob Marley's "Everything's Gonna Be Alright" filtered through the speakers on a loop. They spoke in hushed tones to each other until someone caught sight of the cardboard cut-out of Layton. With all these mourners dressed in black milling around him, Layton's attire seemed especially out of place. His grin suggested he was amused by the inappropriate formality of the space and was trying to make the best of it—maybe he'd even inspire others to loosen up.

Candace sat in an adjoining room with the rest of the family, staring at her hands. Even when overcome with emotion, she had a tendency to clam up if she was in front of other people. Her body's instinct to at least appear calm and composed overrode the one that would trigger tears to well up in her eyes or her lip to tremble. She didn't even cry at her own wedding. And so she was relieved that today's service would be a big, public affair rather than a private ceremony for family. The presence of strangers would help her hold it together.

She didn't want to mingle with anyone before the service began. She needed to go to the bathroom, though, and there was only one, downstairs, which would require walking the gauntlet of people who lined the hallway. People she dreaded

having to see, to make small talk with, to accept hugs and con-
dolences from. And then Rachelle, Matt's wife, went into
mom mode. She told Candace she'd protect her and took her
hand, pulling her sister-in-law through the crowd swiftly, not
giving anyone who wanted to talk to Candace the opportunity to do so.

When all the seats in the chapel had filled, the funeral director, a large man in a jacket that strained across his shoulders,
went to fetch the family. He entered the chapel with Candace
striding in behind him, and everyone rose for her, like they
had on her wedding day. The funeral home had already filled
up the small urn Layton bought for Finn, and some of his ashes
had been given to Willie and Phil. The rest of Layton, the
portion of him that would go into the ground, was in a small
wooden box that Candace was now holding. Friends smiled
encouragingly in her direction, but she focused on the sequence
of actions she had to will her body into performing. *Okay, just
walk a few more steps. Okay, put the box down at the altar. Okay,
make it to your seat now.*

Willie was the first up to speak, and her eyes scanned the
room filled with some of Layton's old classmates, teachers,
former colleagues, and clients, most dressed in black, sitting as
people do at memorial services, solemnly, a box of tissues
never more than a few feet away.

"He would be absolutely mortified to see this crowd,"
Willie said, allowing everyone a release of laughter that lasted
a few beats longer than it might have in any other setting.
They seemed so starved for a bit of levity, a chance to exhale.
"He's gone, but we're here to roast him, I hope. I know there

are a lot of tears, and we're hoping for some laughs as well."

When Candace stepped up, her eyes were swollen behind her glasses, her voice strained both from a cold and from crying. She explained that she was the kind of girl who, if her parents were ten minutes late picking her up from school, would be certain they'd died in a car crash. And then she married a man who, in the last few months of life, would go running with his father. When she'd ask him if he was sure he felt up to it, he'd say, "I'm not dead yet."

Though neither Layton nor Finn were in the room, Candace could feel their presences, and it was like she was speaking to them both at once.

"I promise to always talk to Finn and tell him stories about his dad and how brave and strong and amazing he was. I will see you in Finn every time he's full of anger, excels in sports, or cries because he's sweet and sensitive," she said. "I'll think of you when Joe is on the radio, or any song for that matter. I will laugh whenever Aerosmith is on, thinking of all the 'wahh-kaa-kaas' you used to yell when we'd play their music. No one can ever, ever, ever compare to you. I love you with all my heart, now and forever. I miss you."

Layton's childhood pals fulfilled Willie's request for a roast, cracking a few "that's what she said" jokes in their friend's honour, cursing "the big C"—chlamydia, not cancer—for taking him from them, making a joke about the size of Layton's penis, knowing he wasn't there to volley back with a retort. Before heading back to their seats, they paused to take grinning selfies with the Layton cut-out, like it was a figure at a wax museum, as he'd probably hoped they would.

As Phil stood before a room filled with people grieving his son's death, he said he found comfort in the similarities between his son and Layton's namesake, James Layton Reid, Phil's father, who died in a car crash when Phil was seven years old. They were both moody, sometimes sparing with their words, and liked to expose themselves to danger.

He reflected on how running had brought him and his son together when Layton was an adult. It was Layton who bullied him into running the Boston Marathon before he turned sixty. It was Layton who beat him in a race down the street—barefoot—the night before he started Gerson Therapy. It was Layton who, after completing ten 5K races after he'd done radiation, had said, "How about two more?" He wrapped his eulogy with a spirited reading of "Ulysses" by Tennyson, his fist punching through the air, like a man ready for battle, at the poem's end.

Matt played "You Are My Sunshine" for his grandmother on the piano when she was dying, a performance so moving that Layton asked for a recording of it to put in the Finn Box and requested that his brother play it at his memorial service, so he did.

When Layton planned his backyard vow renewal, he wanted Jenn Grant to sing at it but she was on tour. Later, when he ran into her at the hospital, he told her he would've shot her wedding for free. She sent him a sneak preview of her album, *Paradise*, the follow-up to *Compostela*, before it was released, knowing he might not live to hear it otherwise. And though he wasn't in the room to experience it, she now made his last wish come true: in a cobalt dress, cowboy boots, and a pink and gold three-quarter-sleeve jacket, she stood in front of the room that morning like it was a concert hall at night and played Layton's favourite song.

"Time will take us but cannot break us, time will keep us together. Time will show up in wild roses, I've got a good feeling," she sang soothingly.

hey you guys.

check out this picture i'm using as a metaphor for my future. it's very poetic. that's me wading off into a sunset of uncertainty and darkness and jellyfish. the guy in the photo will most likely make it back to shore safely, but i think you get the point.

remember that time i first told you i had a terminal illness? that was awkward, huh? are you interested in hearing a little bit more about it? alright then.

just over six years ago at a walk-in clinic in ottawa i had a sketchy mole removed from my back which turned out to be melanoma. between 2010 & 2016 i've had five surgeries, tried conventional medication, an intensive two-year natural therapy, yoga, hypnotherapy, meditation, excessive masturbation, scientology, the list goes on. i visited a rogue health clinic in tijuana, mexico with my mom, bathed with a camping shower for a year and a half, sat through thousands of coffee enemas and drank more pressed carrot juices than any one human should consume in their lifetime.

one year ago yesterday, while i was playing with finn in
the backyard i had a seizure, and we discovered a handful
of inoperable brain tumours in my head. fifteen whole-
brain radiotherapy treatments followed by two targeted
stereotactic sessions and we're happy to announce that
i am now 100% tumour free.

just kidding.

still kind of fucked.

but hey, it's ok.

really.

i've had some time to digest all of this, plus we're busy
building a time machine in the backyard so i'm pretty
confident once we get the ball rolling on that we can
still turn this around.

the way i see it is, when confronted with your own
mortality, you've really only got two options. you can
cry and yell and bang your head against the wall in a
fit of fear and frustration and self-pity, or you can wipe
away the tears, pull yourself together, and try to make
as many outlandish demands as possible before people
start to realize you're taking advantage of them.

you've always got a choice, friends. today i choose the
latter.

so, without further adieu i present to you my formal
"i could be dead pretty soon so you better damn well
be nice to me" requests.

serious talk. let's go:

demand #1

i am told (by my wife) that if i give my remains to the
medical student children at dalhousie university, my
body parts will likely be dismembered and discarded
in a dumpster behind a sketchy off-campus fraternity
bar. i'm not sure how reliable this information is, but
if this is the case i would prefer to be cremated. i have
pre-purchased a small urn online. i am told it is possible
to open this urn and retrieve ashes if so desired. if you
or someone you know are planning a trip to antarctica
i strongly suggest you figure out a way to bring my ashes
and spread some of me over there. as you may know,
my only real goal in life, above my career, my wife and
certainly the birth of my son, was to travel and work on
all seven continents before i died. as this is unlikely to
happen at this point (unless our attempts to build a time
machine are successful) it would seem unreasonable of
you not to at least contemplate accommodating this
request. i know what you're thinking and it's not that
cold down there. wear a sweater. additionally, while we're
on the topic of my body parts, in preparation for the
inevitable i have begun collecting toenail clippings (mine)
in a mason jar which will be auctioned off at my funeral
to the highest bidder and/or just gifted to former disgraced
halifax mayor peter kelly.

let me know if you have in mind a specific body part you'd
fancy and i'll see what i can do.

demand #2

just tell her you love her, stupid.

demand #3

eventually there will come a time when you bump into my
son, whether it's on the street or at the grocery store or
in prison. maybe in two years, five years, ten. be cautious
but friendly. approach him slowly and be sure to make
eye-contact. you are to repeat these exact words with the
calmest look your face can muster while maintaining a firm
grip on his left shoulder. "your father loved you more than
you'll ever know." at which point he will nod confidently in
agreement. you'll then whisper "and please wear a condom"
into his right ear before gently cupping the side of his head,
winking once and running off in the opposite direction as
fast as your legs can take you.

demand #4

someone please clear my search browser.

demand #5

my funeral: if available the party will be held at the earl
francis spryfield memorial legion. halifax songstress and
magician jenn grant will be singing "eye of the tiger" or
"barcelona" or whatever else she'd like to sing because it will
be beautiful and poetic and everyone will be so wrapped up
in an emotional and sexual whirlwind of fond memories
of me and my family and "that's what she said" jokes. we
will be serving diagonally sliced wonderbread cucumber
sandwiches with the crust cut off. as jenn is finishing her set

someone who loves me will carry out a life-sized cardboard cutout of my likeness while two dozen white doves are simultaneously released from behind said cardboard cutout. there will also be fireworks. not the dollar store ones, the real ones. perhaps this could be done in the parking lot.

. . .

good grief, that's all i've got for now gang, making demands is exhausting. let's pick this up another day, i haven't even touched on the key party yet.

goodnight my friends.

stay alive.

Xo

seven

The week after the service, Irma was back at work and Candace was on her own—really on her own—for the first time. Though so many of the bureaucratic tasks surrounding death had been taken care of before Layton died, there was still a list to tackle: she had to call the bank, the credit card provider, the passport office, the insurance company. She began so many calls with an exchange of hellos and then, "Yeah, so my husband died a week ago" that the weight of the sentence soon lost its meaning.

By the end of that week, she was aching for a sense of normalcy to return, to be back at work again.

"Are you sure you're ready?" her boss asked.

"I don't know," Candace said. "I won't know till I go back. But I think that I'm ready."

Her colleagues were warm and careful not to bring up the reason for Candace's absence, for which she was grateful. But one woman mentioned it, apologizing for not attending the funeral. Candace smiled and told her it was okay but could feel her stomach turning, her cheeks beginning to burn. *Don't do this*, she thought, but couldn't say. *Don't talk to me about this yet. I can't do this yet.*

While her life had suffered an earthquake, back at the office everything was as it had always been, so she couldn't help but fall back into old patterns. When Layton was alive and she was at work, she'd email him every hour checking in. If he didn't email back, she'd get worried. Then she'd email again and he'd reply, apologizing, explaining he'd been in the shower. It felt strange to do work without distraction. She wanted to check her phone for messages from him, from the oncology team at the hospital, but then realized she didn't need to.

In those first few weeks, it was so hard to be on the phone with insurance claimants whose stories she thought were suspicious, or who she believed were reacting dramatically to small injuries. She fantasized sometimes about screaming at them, "You're saying your arm hurts? I'm sorry that your arm hurts, but it doesn't mean you can't work. My husband just died!"

·

Willie and Phil turned inwards during the coldest months, holed up at home with cups of hot coffee, Danish noir films, and a steady soundtrack of public radio. They had been accustomed to getting together on Friday nights with a group of the neighbours to chat about politics or neighbourhood gossip, but after Layton's death, those get-togethers became unbearable. They'd sit around in a circle at someone's house and people would start asking them in concerned whispers, "Oh, how are you doing?" in a way that carried more gravity than when a bank teller or supermarket cashier asked. Sometimes, Willie wanted to snap back, "How the fuck do you think we're doing?" Their answers were ever-evolving and it sort of became a game, finding inventive ways to reply to such an impossible question. Phil's go-to had become a very British, uncertain, "Okay, I think."

There were others who would come to visit but would brag about the vacations they were about to take, which Willie and Phil didn't have the patience for. Their social network grew smaller, to include only their closest friends. They were living quietly, isolating themselves during a time of year when it was socially acceptable to do so. They soon found it easier to stay at home on Friday nights in the safety of each other's company.

When spring came, Willie found it painful to watch everything coming to life again, to see baby ducks at the pond near Layton's house. These were reminders of what she didn't have. Soon after Layton's memorial service, Willie, Phil, and Candace agreed that they'd wait until the spring, when the ground had thawed, to bury Layton's remains. It was gutting for Willie to realize they'd be putting Layton into the earth but that nothing would sprout from there.

The day before the planned burial, Willie, Phil, and Matt's son Trevor set out early to the town of Caribou on the Northumberland Strait, where a friend had offered up her house for the weekend. It was a half-hour drive from Thorburn, where Willie's parents were buried and Layton would soon be too. Phil felt some apprehension on the drive: he'd already said a painful goodbye to his son, and this was reopening that wound. He described Layton's death like a merry-go-round stopping: they needed to get off and move on. Hopefully this would allow them to.

The three spent the night at the house and the next day, after noon, met with Candace, Finn, Candace's parents, Matt, his wife, Rachelle, and their other son, Mitchell, at the cemetery. It was a frigid day and everyone was a little underdressed. The children raced between the headstones, giggling, while the adults huddled around the hole that had been dug up beside Willie's parents' plots, a foot from Layton's newly laid headstone. What he'd ultimately chosen was exactly what he was looking for. It was small, shiny, black, and to the point. No engraved flowers or ostentatious serif fonts. No quotes or lines of poetry. All that was missing was the engraving of his year of death.

REID

LAYTON ALEXANDER

1979

A GOOD LIFE

The children were corralled and briefed on what was happening. "Why didn't we do this the day after Uncle Layton died?" Mitchell asked.

"It was winter and cold and we wanted to wait till the weather was warmer," Willie explained.

She'd brought a dozen roses with her—one for each person to throw into the freshly dug earth and one to place on each of her parents' graves. Candace stood quietly, clutching the box with Layton's ashes, her lips blue from the cold.

"So, how would you like to do this?" Willie asked.

Candace explained there was to be no formality; that wasn't what Layton would want. "Don't we have to wait for the cemetery guy to come cover it up?" she asked.

"Oh no, he'll be by later," Willie said.

Candace knelt to place Layton's ashes in the ground, and then everyone tossed in a rose. Before she stood up, Candace pressed her lips to the smooth, cold headstone.

"Kiss the headstone," she instructed Finn. "This is where Daddy's going to be."

"No no, I don't want to do that!" Finn shrieked and tore off again with his cousins.

And then it was over. They got into their cars and drove as a convoy to the house in Caribou, where Willie got started on dinner. While their children played together, Candace and Rachelle began a massive puzzle, popping open a mid-afternoon bottle of wine. As Matt walked into the house, he noticed a zucchini on the kitchen table with two avocados arranged at one end and laughed at this vulgar little joke his brother certainly would've made if he were there. "I had to leave a little nod to Layton. A little bit of rudery," Willie said, revealing herself as the artist.

She prepared one of Layton's favourite meals in his honour: a seventeen-pound turkey with gravy and sausage stuffing, the same she'd made at his final Christmas. There were cupcakes for dessert. As they sat down, it dawned on Willie that this might be a time when they would go around the table and reflect on what they missed about Layton. But before she could suggest it aloud, she immediately dismissed the idea in her head, thinking, *That is so fucking staged and Layton would hate it.*

Instead, the rest of the weekend turned into a simple family retreat. They finished the puzzle, the boys ran outside, face-planting in the mud. In the morning, Matt read them stories while Irma and Candace made waffles with blueberries for the group. Then they capped the day off with a walk along the beach, everyone in windbreakers and boots, the wind whipping through their hair.

·

Willie occasionally spoke to Layton when she was alone. She'd say, "Oh, Layton, why'd you do this?" Sometimes, on a walk in the park, a feather would float by or a butterfly would slow down its journey and dart around her face and she'd whisper, "Oh hey, hi," to it, certain it was a manifestation of her son. In all her dreams of Layton, he was in the last stages of his life and she was caring for him. She would stand at his bedside and tell him, "Let go, please let go." It wasn't revisiting trauma in any way to have these dreams—she'd wake up from them feeling warm and comforted.

At the theatre where Phil volunteered, they were going to stage *Double Indemnity* and the director offered Phil the lead role. The character was in nearly every scene and saying yes would require a big time commitment—and now Phil had nothing but time. He told the director he was leaning towards saying yes but then awoke one night with a sinking feeling. *Christ, I'm not ready for this*, he thought, and bailed.

After much back and forth, they planned a summer trip to Rochester to see Willie's sister—their first time leaving the province in five years—and then another one to Darbyshire in the U.K. to see Phil's family. Since Layton's death, all the trips they'd taken were short getaways, like overnights to the Annapolis Valley a few hours' drive away. Willie and Phil had intended for these to be short vacations from their mourning— like they could put their feelings on hold if they travelled, say, more than a hundred kilometres from where their son had died. But when they arrived at their destination, Willie would unpack her clothes and there would be her grief tucked in a corner of the suitcase: still waiting for her. When Candace floated the idea of renting a house in Florida for her and Finn to escape to for a few weeks after Layton's death, Willie told her, "The pain goes with you." Candace took that advice and stayed in Halifax. At least at home, she could clean or keep busy with work to distract herself. On vacation, her mind would be more free, she'd have more time to dwell on her loss.

She and Layton's parents didn't talk about Layton all that much—they tiptoed around the subject of this monumental loss they'd experienced, not wanting to force the other to take on someone else's grief burden in addition to their own. Candace assumed Willie and Phil avoided bringing Layton up because they were thinking, *She's got enough on her own to deal with. We're not going to be like, "Oh, we're having a hard time with this."*

None gave much thought to what their relationship to each other would look like now that Layton was gone—the mere existence of Finn bonded them. And to Layton's parents, Candace very much still felt like their daughter. In May, Candace and Willie stood side-by-side at a Jenn Grant show. On a visit the singer had made to the house a few months earlier, Willie and Jenn spoke about the track "Dogfight" and how Layton was one of the inspirations behind it: *I've been all over, I've been all over this world. But I still can't save ya.* That night at the show, before she sang the song live, she looked at the crowd and said, "This is for Layton's mom," and Candace elbowed Willie, grinning.

Every Tuesday, while Candace was at work, Willie and Phil stopped by the house for an hour to walk Gracie and put food in the fridge—some veggie burgers or soup or a casserole that would cover off dinner that night and usually the next as well. For weeks, Willie insisted her daughter-in-law leave the previous day's dishes out for her to wash, until Candace finally acquiesced. On Wednesdays, when Phil volunteered at the theatre, he'd stop in again to feed and walk Gracie. In the summer, they mowed the lawn, laid down sod, and tended to the garden, as they had when Layton was still at home. They saw Finn frequently. It was nice to have this routine now. In the first few weeks after Layton died, they didn't see much of their grandson. He was confused by this change and clung to his mother, his pillar, not wanting to be left alone with anyone else.

At Willie and Phil's house, some of Layton's remains were kept in a small mason jar nestled beside one of Phil's big rubber boots, balanced on a window frame along the stairs to the basement. Phil had scooped them out of the box Candace had, wanting to keep a small portion aside to sprinkle in the dirt when they planted a sapling in their backyard that spring. There was some left over, which they kept on the off chance any of Layton's friends ever did make it to Antarctica.

By the summertime, their memories of their son were fading, and it saddened Willie that the sharp image she'd once had of Layton—down to the lines in his face and his exact stature—had now blurred. If a day went by without her thinking about him, she wondered, *Is something wrong with me?*

Phil had had a different experience. In the first few months, he would push back his grief when it started to rise up, like plugging a drain. But later, he learned the value of leaning into it, letting it wash over him. After he reached this point of acceptance, the memories of Layton weren't as jarring or painful as they had been. There were moments when Finn's expression or laugh or frenzied dancing would remind Phil of what Layton was like at that age. Grief, he learned, was a funny thing, and sometimes one to be welcomed. There were situations he put himself in that would force him to think of his son, like the 5K races he continued to do with Candace, Irma, Matt, and some of Layton's friends. Sometimes, he'd see Layton jogging beside him, a slow shuffle, responding to Phil's questions in the non-communicative grunts he'd used as a teenager.

·

Candace often thought back to how, when they were deciding whether or not to keep Layton in the palliative care ward, Layton had asked her if dying in the house would ruin it for her. At the time, she'd insisted it wouldn't, but the truth was she didn't know how else to answer. She wouldn't know how the house would feel after he was gone until he was actually gone. In the weeks after Layton died she looked at real estate listings online, but nothing interested her. The house didn't feel empty like she feared. It was comforting. This was the only place other than where she grew up that felt like home. Layton's room was a warm and cozy space, but she also felt like it was frozen in time, and if she studied things too long, those comforts saddened her. The room was a reminder more of Layton on Gerson than of Layton dying: the room, that bed, those shelves, the juice stains on everything. She didn't want to think about that time anymore. In the fog of the first week after he was gone, she had to freeze her heart and take on the task like she was a third party. She started with swapping out the duvet cover. Then came the closet. She couldn't stand seeing his clothes in there. She went through each shirt and pair of pants methodically, trashing most of them but setting aside in a plastic bin a few items she thought Finn might like one day. She kept a T-shirt and two hoodies for herself in the closet, but soon realized even that was too painful and got rid of them.

There were heaps of unused medical supplies—maybe a thousand dollars' worth, she estimated. She called around to hospitals and pharmacies, but all refused them for liability reasons. She finally found a willing recipient in an animal shelter. Layton's desk was filled with things: stationery, rubber stamps he'd made. None of it was deeply personal, but Candace was on a mission to cleanse the space. Knowing some of the items might be useful, she packed them away. What was important was getting them out of that room. The one item that gave her pause was Layton's camera. Long before he died, he had instructed her to sell it after he was gone. He estimated she'd get about a thousand dollars for it. He pleaded with her not to hold on to it, reminding her she'd never pick it up and that it was foolish to save it for Finn, as the technology would be ancient by the time he was old enough to use it. But more than even his clothes, to Candace this camera always seemed like an appendage of Layton. Tossing it felt like tossing out a piece of him. She was just thankful his most beloved strap, the checkered one, had broken and had been replaced before he died. She knew it would be too hard to see that strap, even though the camera sat in the closet. When he came home after a sixteen-hour wedding shoot, carrying the camera in his hand—that cheery strap dangling from it—he'd place it on the kitchen table and then collapse on the couch before making his way up the stairs to bed, where Candace was usually already asleep. When the Gerson schedule eased up, giving them a two-hour window to go to the park, Candace would push Finn in his stroller and Layton would walk a few paces behind sometimes, his camera slung around his neck by that damn strap, the shutter snapping rapidly—click, click, click, click, click—as he captured his two favourite subjects.

When April hit, Candace decided it was time for a bigger change—she switched rooms with Finn. It was an easy sell for Finn: an upgrade to the bigger room where he'd have more space for his big-boy bed and all his toys. The switch involved cleaning out what was in all the drawers underneath the bed in the room she shared with Layton, which contained stacks of medical files. They all had "CAPITAL HEALTH" as their header and were filled with the medical jargon that spelled out the mounting horrors Layton's body had endured in his final years. *I can't look at this. I don't want this in the house,* Candace thought when she unearthed them. She started a fire in the wood stove and threw them all in, watching with satisfaction as the flames hungrily inhaled them, reducing them to ash.

But even the room change wasn't dramatic enough. Two weeks after Layton's death, once she'd decided she wanted to stay in the house, she made moves on a long-held dream to renovate. It was something she'd wanted for years but could never justify when Layton was alive. She longed for a brand-new kitchen with smart grey cabinets and stainless steel appliances. She planned to replace the floors. She wanted to add an extra room and bathroom to the main floor. She dreamed of painting the house's exterior a charcoal grey. A home equity loan plus the money from Layton's life insurance payout and the inheritance from his grandmother would make it all possible.

At first, she was certain what Layton would say if he were there, watching her make these plans: "Candace, what are you doing?! Don't spend all your money." But then she came to believe he would be happy to see that the money was going to the house he loved so much—that it was allowing them to stay in it. Layton had fallen in love with how it was so much like a little cabin in the city, and though this renovation would give the space a more modern look, Candace wanted to preserve its cottagey charms by keeping the wood stove and adding exposed beams and stained wood planks. She felt that focusing so much energy and attention on this was what got her through the first six months without Layton—that, and exercise.

Immediately after Layton's death, Candace had a full plate. She'd returned to work, she was taking care of long-shelved tasks at home, she was ferrying Finn to daycare and extra-curriculars, she was planning a major renovation, she was doing all those five-kilometre races. As Irma watched, she worried that her daughter might not be taking enough time to grieve properly. She knew Candace had had a lot of time to come to terms with what her life without Layton would be like before he died, but she wondered if her daughter was trying to busy herself now in order to avoid thinking about it. She didn't want to interfere because she knew Candace had to make decisions on her own. Irma sometimes offered her opinions to her daughter, but they weren't always welcome. She also realized that maybe this was what her daughter needed: after three and a half years of putting her own needs and desires second, of having so much of her life revolve around making sure things ran smoothly at home, she was suddenly gifted with the luxury of time and freedom to do whatever she wanted. To be selfish.

What others didn't realize was that Candace had those chances for reflection all the time, and sometimes they were suffocating. She'd been running the household on her own for so long that not much changed, in a practical sense, once Layton was gone. But she found herself missing him in the smallest moments: when a lightbulb went out or the batteries died in the smoke detector, she couldn't ask him to take care of it—she'd have to get up on a chair and do it herself. She felt his absence nearly every day around suppertime. No matter how busy her schedule was, it was the moment when she sat down to eat dinner that marked the start of family time. Layton, even if he'd spent the whole day in bed, would descend the stairs and pull up a chair at the table alongside Finn and Candace. After that last trip home from the hospital, Candace felt the loss acutely because Layton was now taking all of his meals in his room, too weak to join them. There was no slow shuffle down the lemon-coloured stairs. His absence after his death was so palpable, so devastating, that Candace decided to start new traditions with Finn. She'd put some music on her phone so they'd be serenaded while they ate their chicken and rice and vegetables. Or they'd have dance parties in the kitchen, Finn's arms flailing, his hands slapping his belly and thighs to the beat of the song, or sometimes to an even more frenetic beat he heard in his own head.

The decision to be this way wasn't only about Candace. She wanted to be emotionally healthy for Finn. She didn't want her son to come home to a mom who was crying. It would be exhausting for the both of them if she was upset all the time. She spent her days at work talking to people who were going through a lot of distress, which is precisely why she didn't want to dwell on that stuff when she left the office. Sometimes, she'd wake up in the morning and struggle to face the day, so she got into a routine with Finn and her mother. "I'm going to have a good day today. Are you going to have a good day today?" she'd ask.

Finn, grinning, would often say, "I'm going to have a good day today."

Other mornings he was grumpy. "I'm not going to today," he'd proclaim with a pout. But then Irma would chirp up that she was going to have a good day, and the two women, with forced smiles they willed into being real ones, would get Finn to reluctantly agree.

Candace and Irma were convinced Layton was out there somewhere, in some form, and he let them know with dimes. They were never quarters or nickels—only dimes. The coins would catch their eye, glinting on the ground on the sidewalk, or on the asphalt in a parking lot. They'd never noticed them before Layton was gone, but now they seemed to find them everywhere.

After one particular evening out with her sisters, Irma was feeling upset about Layton's death and returned home. She went to the record player, where she found Elton John's Greatest Hits record uncharacteristically sitting out, an album Finn loved bopping around to, and when she went to put it in its sleeve, she found a dime inside. This discovery felt like a gentle hug from Layton, a little *I'm still here with you.*

Another day, she had to get fingerprinted to get security clearance at work, and afterwards, when getting into her car, she found a dime. It wouldn't have had any significance if she'd found it a year earlier, but in this moment, she figured her son-in-law was trying to say something sarcastic to her—this was where he'd drop the witty one-liner about how she was secretly a spy or a criminal, she thought.

Candace knew there were support groups for widows out there, but wading through the muck of grief with others who were feeling the same way held no appeal. If she was already feeling miserable, why did she want to go to this space and hear about how other people were also miserable? She felt the same way that Layton did about all those cancer support groups he refused to attend when he was alive. If she was going to talk to a widow, she wanted that person to be someone who was on the other side, someone who had been widowed for a decade or more, someone who had all the answers.

While she waited for the summer to come, when construction could begin, Candace ordered furniture for her new bedroom and put down a new coat of paint. The second floor felt refreshed. Now, to decorate the walls. For months, a plastic bin sat at the foot of her bed with framed art in it, mostly family photos shot by Layton, or portraits from their wedding. She'd revisit them again and again, unable to decide if they should go up. She wanted to meet someone new and get married again; it didn't feel right to have these photos of her dead husband on the walls.

By July, it dawned on her that this was the longest point since she had first started dating in high school that she'd been single. She'd found herself surprised when she'd get a bit nervous before the contractor would come by the house, until she realized what she was experiencing was a crush. He was tall and skinny, like Layton. When she described him, she smiled widely, exposing her back teeth, her cheeks giving way to dimples. He was a few years younger than her and not even a real prospect anyway because he was in a relationship, but the simple feeling of being attracted to someone was a cheap and welcome thrill. She liked having a crush. She liked the feeling of the circuitry inside her working again. She'd recently come into the time where she didn't feel like she was living her old life, or where missing Layton made up so much of her day.

At one point, when he was at home and a young doctor made a house call, Layton took notice of how handsome he was. *This guy is good enough for Candace*, he thought. After the doctor had finished his assessment of Layton and was walking out of the room, Layton called out to him. "Excuse me, there's one more thing," he said and pointed over to Candace, who was in the next room, and wiggled his eyebrows suggestively. The doctor (who it turned out was already in a relationship) laughed. Layton loved seeing what kinds of things a dying man could get away with.

Willie wasn't sure if it was okay for her to bring the subject up with Candace, but she thought it was important to be upfront about it. "When the grief subsides and you want to find somebody to love, please don't feel like we're ever watching over, going, 'Oh, he won't work,'" she told Candace. And Candace nodded, not wanting to reveal quite yet to her mother-in-law that this was already on her mind since Layton had brought it up so much in the last year and a half of his life. He had told her again and again she needed to live her own life; he'd given her not only his permission but his enthusiastic encouragement.

A month after Layton died, Candace stopped wearing her wedding ring. Keeping it on was more painful than taking it off. This wasn't her life anymore. She wasn't married anymore.

It was a harsh thing to think, but also the truth. Right after losing Layton, she'd worn his wedding ring on her middle finger. A few months before his death, Layton had given it to Irma to take to the jewellery store to engrave with "You got this" in tiny, almost illegible text, knowing it would be left as a gift for Candace. Till the end, that phrase was a joke between them after she, having run out of truly inspirational messages to put on the fridge, put that one on a Post-it. After a few weeks, she removed Layton's ring and put it in her jewellery box, and soon it was joined by her own wedding ring. On her left ring finger, where there had been a band of gold with a white cameo of a woman on a peach-coloured background, there was now a band of smooth skin exposed for the first time in a long time. But soon enough the naked finger would be just another finger. This marker on her body, signifying that she was married and then not, would fade.

Candace had recently heard about a dating app in which, after two people matched, it was up to the woman to send the first message to the man. This seemed like a good place to start for her, but she didn't know which pictures to use. Of course there were hundreds, if not thousands, that Layton had taken that would be perfect profile picture material—her dimpled smile naturally captured, the golden hour light putting a warm halo around her hair—but it felt wrong somehow to use one of those portraits her dead husband had so lovingly shot to attract a new man. Eventually, she settled on a few selfies she'd saved on her phone. She immediately felt overwhelmed by the app as profiles appeared on it. How could you tell whether or not you'd have chemistry with someone by looking at a few photos of them? Some guys posted pictures of their dog, or of themselves posing with a woman. What did this mean? She felt like she'd stepped out of a time machine. Her first night using the app, she swiped left on every man's profile that popped up—rejecting them all. The next day she took her profile down. She wasn't ready for this.

Dating was intimidating, not only because she'd been out of the game for so long—she'd been with Layton for seventeen years—but because she'd never really even been in the game. She'd never had a one-night stand, never casually dated. She'd only ever slept with four people and she'd been in serious relationships with all of them, one after another. Her younger colleagues told her that apps were the only way people met now—there was no meeting at parties or at clubs anymore, a fact that confounded Candace.

But maybe this was time for a new Candace, she thought. For a long time, when others would describe her as "sweet" she would take it as a compliment, but now that description irked her. Even before Layton, she felt like she had always been a bit of a pushover, the kind of woman who never did anything without carefully calculating what other people would think, always wanting to please others before herself. She was very much the opposite of her husband, and now felt like she owed it to him to live a little more in his spirit, to be a little selfish and independent.

Soon after she returned to work, she set the wheels in motion to make the switch from covering short-term disability cases to long-term ones—something she'd wanted for a while but had never had the time to commit to when Layton was sick.

Early on a Saturday in July, Candace decided to try another way of being the new version of herself. She hadn't ever been much of a joiner at the office: when colleagues her age would go out for happy hour drinks, she would pick up Finn from daycare and drive home. She had a sick husband to return to and nobody ever hassled her about it. When the people putting office teams together for the city's annual dragon boat race asked her to participate that year, she didn't have a good reason to say no. Maybe Candace 2.0 should expand her friend circle a little, get to know her colleagues more, she thought. Maybe she would . . . have fun? The morning of the race, she drove to Lake Banook, where the fog was so thick it made it hard to tell exactly where the sky ended and the lake began. Candace dressed like everyone else there that day, in a baseball cap and athletic gear—but she'd swiped a bit of mascara on, too.

The fog lifted and resettled every few minutes, vaporizing as quickly as it had appeared, masking and then shrouding all the houses that dotted the waterfront. Candace was at ease with her colleagues, seeing many of them for the first time outside of the office. There were little in-jokes she was beginning to understand, a familiarity she could have with individuals who until this point had been nothing more than people she worked alongside. A few asked if she would be joining them for a drink later and she declined, but it was only because Candace 2.0 already had evening plans.

Her best friend had mentioned that a DJ they liked would be doing a set at a club downtown that night. They could dance, they could drink, it would be a nice release for her, her friend said. So she agreed. After leaving Irma at the house to look

after Finn, Candace and her friend arrived at the club at 10:30—
it had been a while since the two of them, both mothers, had
been part of this scene, and they'd forgotten how early this
was. After a while, a man came over to buy Candace a drink,
and for the first time in her life, she let him. He looked younger
than her, but she couldn't tell by how much. He asked her what
her story was, in that light, flirtatious way he probably had
dozens of times before with other women, maybe expecting
her to list where she'd grown up, what she did for a living.

"Oh, you don't want to know, it's too sad," she told him,
giggling nervously. But he was pushy. She kept insisting it was
too much, so he started guessing. Was she married? Did she
have kids? Candace laughed at how decidedly unscandalous
these things were; this poor guy was too young and innocent
to even imagine what had actually happened to her. Finally,
she dumped the truth on him—she was a widow, her husband
had died of cancer earlier that year. He was sympathetic, but
undeterred. They continued chatting.

At 1 a.m., she texted her mother to tell her she was getting
into a cab. But then, she indulged in a few more last drinks and
dances and the minutes slipped away. In the back seat of the cab
on the way to her house, Candace made out with this stranger,
who didn't know her as Candace, Layton's poor widow, or
Candace, Layton's selfless wife, but as Candace, that fun, flirtatious woman at the club. She felt light and unburdened for the
first time in a long time. She gave the man her number and,
smiling, walked into the house at 3 a.m.

She flipped off her wedge heels to give her aching feet, which
were most often in sneakers or Birkenstocks, a rest and then

giddily recounted the night to her mother in whispers like they were college roommates. Irma was excited to see this version of her daughter again, but privately hoped this was just fun—she believed it was too soon for Candace to get into a serious relationship.

The next morning, Candace was hungover for the first time in a long time and her appetite was shot. She made a smoothie but managed to take only a few sips of it and put the rest in the fridge. She'd already exchanged a few text messages with the man from the night before and was planning to see him again later in the week. A few minutes past noon, Finn, who was none the wiser about his mother's night out, sat content in front of an iPad watching *Paw Patrol* as he ate noodles and vegetables in a bowl. That morning, Candace let him watch an extra episode—she was too exhausted to fight him on it.

For a while after Layton died, Candace, like Willie, found herself speaking to him—both in her head and aloud. She had a few visitation dreams, but by summer they stopped. She hated this, and on particularly difficult days, she'd lie in bed staring at the ceiling, willing him to appear to her after she dozed off. "Please come visit me. Please talk to me," she begged. But it never worked. She still had one-sided conversations with him during the day, but even those became less frequent. She hadn't yet had a chance to tell Layton about the new guy she'd met, but she wasn't nervous about it. She'd already confessed to him the moment she realized she was ready to start dating again. "I wish you were here. I wish it was you," she told him. She was certain he knew that, but it made her feel more at peace to articulate it aloud.

She Googled "how to date after widowhood" and unearthed blogs written by women in their thirties, forties, and fifties about their experience. Some began a few weeks after losing their partners; others took months or years. This comforted her. Reading these accounts, she saw her loss as easier than some others'. She compared herself to women who lost their husbands at war. Their loss was sudden, unexpected, and it seemed like their grief was murkier, deeper, and took much longer to plod through. Candace, meanwhile, felt she had been blessed, in some sense, with years to grieve, and she'd had Layton to navigate that grief with. There were no regrets, no sentiments left unexpressed, no final "I love yous" she felt cheated out of. When he'd returned home from the hospital to die, he wasn't the same old Layton anymore—he was a rough outline of himself, an approximation. His humour, his personality, his essence had been zapped from him, so she let go of him then. And in the weeks that followed, she already felt like a widow, even though Layton's heart was technically still beating.

But she also wondered if she was giving herself too much credit—maybe, like with work, she felt more ready than she was. She wondered if she was bottling up her feelings in a way she didn't realize, that maybe the first time she was intimate with a new man, they would be unleashed in a messy torrent. What if she started crying, she wondered, and didn't know how to stop?

·

A few months after Layton died, Candace's parents bought a house in Halifax a few minutes' drive from their daughter's. They were driving one day in their neighbourhood with Finn when they saw a little boy crossing the street. They braked to let him cross safely and Finn studied him from the back seat. "I wonder if that little boy's family is all dead," Finn said. Preschooler logic had suggested that if you were alone, it meant everyone you knew had died. Irma was stunned by the statement, but was quick to reassure him: "No, he's just going home after visiting with his friends."

In the months following Layton's death, when anyone entered Finn's room, he'd show them the cut-out of Layton from the memorial service that now had a permanent place there—Willie liked to say Layton was guarding over the space. When Finn gave visitors a tour, he'd end it by closing the door, revealing the cut-out, and earnestly explaining, "You know, my daddy died."

Irma always took this as an opportunity. "Yes Finn, I know," she would say. "Daddy died. He loved you very much and we're never going to forget him."

But there was a fear that Finn would. Irma made a habit of showing him photos of himself and his father on her phone, to take advantage of moments that reminded her of Layton and share those stories with her grandson. She decorated the room in her house that Finn slept in when he stayed overnight with photos of him with his father.

Phil lost his father in a car crash when he was seven and has very few memories of him compared to his brother, who was ten at the time. As a result, the two boys processed the death very differently: his brother became obsessed with finding out more about his father's life, a kind of rabid curiosity that Phil never felt pulled by in the same way. After Layton's memorial service, Phil spoke to his brother and said, "You know, I don't remember much about Daddy's funeral." His brother laughed. "You weren't there, Phil." Phil came to see it as a blessing, in some sense, that Finn lost his father at such a young age. It was hard to know at this point how much Finn would want to know about Layton. Would he be curious? Would it be easier if he wasn't?

When Willie and Phil looked after their grandson, they'd let him take the lead on talking about Layton. Opportunities would arise, but they were fleeting. "My dad died and I'm very sad," he'd say thoughtfully to one of his grandparents, and then rush across the room to pick up a new toy.

Candace was reassured, though. Nearly a year before he died, in the spring, Layton was digging in the garden with Finn when they unearthed a small, white marble. It soon became a favourite possession of Finn's, and now nearly a year after Layton's death, Finn still played with it, sending it rolling down tall contraptions he built in the living room. There were little stories he'd pipe up with from time to time about his father that would catch Candace off guard. One afternoon, when I was visiting, Finn and I sat in the living room together as I helped him construct a winding track. "Daddy was good at wooden trains," he told me in a show-offy tone, like he was describing his favourite superhero from a cartoon. Later, he raved, "Daddy was so tall, so when I was a baby, he used to pull me in a frying pan like a truck!"

"Did someone tell you that about Daddy?" Candace asked, and Finn insisted these were things he remembered.

Candace began to notice that Finn's toughest days always followed the ones in which he spent time with Layton's male friends, many of whom had a similar temperament to Layton. The day after, Finn would complain to Candace, seemingly out of the blue, "I miss Daddy." It was like the visits with those men had triggered memories in Finn: *Oh, this is what it was like to have a father.* Like he hadn't noticed anything was missing from his life until he spent a few hours with men like this.

After Layton died, people recommended books to Candace that were meant to help explain death to a child. The one that got to Candace the most was *Ida, Always*, about two polar bears at the Central Park Zoo. Ida becomes incurably ill and Gus watches what this does to her. They can no longer play like they once did; Ida is often too tired or not in the mood. Sometimes, she needs days on her own, and Gus does too. And then one day, she doesn't come out of her cave at all.

When Candace read it to Finn, it wasn't like some of his other picture books, which she could speed through. Its bare but evocative descriptions told a story that mirrored what happened in her life. Layton was Ida. She was Gus. Her voice cracked sometimes when she read it, and she had to pause to collect herself. She'd never cried while reading it to Finn, or at least not that he'd noticed, but he could pick up on how difficult it was for his mother.

"This is a really sad book," Finn told me one day when he

noticed me pick it up, studying the painted polar bears cuddling up together on the cover. "Mommy makes it sad."

"I don't make it sad!" Candace protested. "It *is* sad."

•

In the late summer, before the big renovation began, the contractor noticed an issue with the bathroom pipes and broke the bad news to Candace: to fix it would add at least another ten thousand dollars to her bill, which was already stretching past her budget. She decided to ditch the whole plan for the renovation and instead concentrate her efforts on sprucing up the main floor: maybe she'd get new countertops for the kitchen, finally toss out the big sectional she had slept on so many nights during Layton's last few years and buy a nice leather sofa, some chairs, a proper coffee table. Maybe a refresh was all she needed for now.

It was a relief to Willie, who had bitten her tongue many times when Candace had excitedly described her plans for the renovation. She, like Candace, could hear her Layton's voice in her head, saying, "Candace, slow down," or warning that the construction would likely linger into the fall.

Half a year later, it became a relief to Candace, too. On a day in late January, a year after Layton died, Halifax received a heavy dump of snow. Preschool had been cancelled for the day for Finn, so Candace had decided to work from home. At lunch, the two went outside—she to shovel, he to play—and Candace realized something. This was a classic Maritime winter day and Finn shouldn't be keeping his mother company while she shovelled—he should be building snow forts or snowmen with the other kids in the neighbourhood, running around like a maniac, working up a sweat while bundled up in his winter gear. The next week, she said it aloud to herself: "It's time." She wanted to live in a kid-friendly neighbourhood, with a sidewalk. She wanted Finn to have the same childhood she and Layton had enjoyed.

In the spring, Candace decided, she'd list the house for sale and look for a new place in her parents' neighbourhood, which was a few minutes away and right beside the school where Finn would be starting in the fall. It would be a three-bedroom house—maybe she'd turn the third room into a gym, with a treadmill. It felt like fate that the renovation had fallen through. She knew she'd have been stuck there for a long time, unable to bring herself to move since it would have meant taking a huge loss on her investment.

Aside from wanting a different childhood experience for her son, Candace simply felt the house was holding her back from moving on. She'd transformed the second floor, but the main one still triggered her. The kitchen floor reminded her of the first time Layton had a seizure, right in front of the sink, which led to the discovery of his brain tumours. When she looked out the window into the yard, she remembered the times Layton wordlessly came down the stairs, walked out the door and lay under a tree. Sometimes, he'd be in the kind of pain that made it difficult to talk, and stretching out on the grass was the only thing that brought him calm. Other times, chills would take over his body and he was desperate for the warmth of the sun. He'd lie outside with his arms and legs covered and pull his hood up over his head, sunbathing in the only way he could.

•

In those final weeks before he lost consciousness, Layton gave Irma a letter in a sealed envelope and asked that his mother-in-law deliver the letter to Candace on the day he died. In it, he thanked Candace for the life they'd had together, for pushing him to do things he wasn't ready to do at the time, things that resulted in him dying at peace with how he'd lived.

In the fall, Layton confessed to Candace he felt bad that he'd spent so much time and energy on the Finn Box, not thinking of her.

"What can I do for you? What can I leave you?" he asked.

"Don't worry about it," she reassured him. "We've had all those conversations. Don't stress about it. I just need you to tell me things are going to be fine."

A month after his death, a second Layton letter arrived. There was no stamp on it—it simply appeared in the box the day Candace came home from work. On the envelope was written, "you got this," the phrase that had evolved from joke to genuine reassurance—exactly what she'd asked him for.

Inside was a Polaroid photo of Layton and Finn together and a quote. Candace wept as she read it. Layton had left a year's worth of these—each with a new photo and quote, all in a "you got this" envelope—with Irma, along with instructions that they be delivered to Candace's mailbox on the anniversary of his death each month.

He had planned to write letters initially, asking close friends for prompts on what sort of greeting they might take comfort in receiving from him after he was gone. Pared-down messages reiterating his feelings for his wife? Slightly sardonic poetry? Recaps of his happiest memories with her? He had put pen to paper so many times, but as the cancer took over his neural function, he'd forget what he'd intended to write. Or he'd sit down with a clear objective but learn that his once-rich vocabulary had been ransacked by the army of tumours in his brain. He tried to summon words or turns of phrase he knew would best express what he wanted to say, but they would vaporize between his fingers before he could grab them. In the end, defeated, he relied on passages written by others that spoke to him and better articulated what his brain could not.

Every month, as the nineteenth drew near, Candace grew excited in anticipation of another letter. If she saw her mother the day before, she'd remind her. The letters helped transport her back to the earlier days of their relationship—before Layton's sickness had consumed their lives. It was a nice way to reset her memories of him. When she read and reread them, she could hear his voice in her head.

She knew there was a finite number of letters, and as the new year drew closer, she dreaded the day when she'd receive her last one. But she knew that even if they kept coming for another year, or five more, there would never be enough. And she also recognized that the temporary soothing they offered her was often followed by pain, like lifting the corner of a scab that was so close to healing over.

In the new year, Candace decided she needed a break from

dating—or at least from actively seeking someone to date. No apps, no dating websites, no set-ups. She'd had a fun fling with the guy she'd met at the club, never growing too committed because she knew he'd be leaving at the end of the summer. There was no hurtful breakup, just two people who liked—but didn't love—each other, parting ways after a few fun months together. But the dating experiments that followed were stressful or disappointing. She didn't have the time or energy for that. The only thing that gave her pause was what this would mean for Finn. It had been easy enough raising a little boy by herself, but she wondered what would happen next, as her son was now at the age where he might soon be asking uncomfortable questions about his body that she felt ill-equipped to answer. It would be nice to have a man around for that—someone who wasn't a grandfather but a partner, a person she could pose questions to and get the right answers from. Or, better yet, someone who could speak to Finn directly. But getting there felt like something far in the distance. For now, she would have to be enough for her son.

On a Sunday trip to Point Pleasant Park, Finn had been whining for two tiresome minutes about how he needed to go to the bathroom until Candace, pushing the buggy he rode in with Gracie trotting along a few paces ahead, pulled up to one. Finn was still young enough that Candace could go into the restroom with him without anyone making a fuss about it. After the toilet flushed, she told him, as she always did, "Okay, Finnie, now wash your hands."

"But I don't want to," he said, summoning his whiniest tone again.

"You have to," she said, her voice revealing this was a conversation they'd had many times before.

"But it's so *boring*!" he protested.

The standoff ended. The faucet turned on. Finn emerged from the bathroom, wiping his wet hands on his thighs, Candace right behind him. As Candace untangled Gracie's leash and steered the buggy back onto the path, Finn ran ahead of her. This path was where Layton raced his brother when they were kids, where he trained for cross-country runs as a teenager, where he and Candace walked their new puppy, where, a year before he died, he ran a 5K surrounded by puddles, mud-flecked snow, and naked trees. Finn was built just like Layton was when he was a kid, and he moved in the same way when he ran: his long, thin legs and gangly arms bouncing wildly, not following any clear kinetic pattern. He wasn't quite used to his body yet, but he knew he had to keep moving.

acknowledgements

Thank you to my unbelievably loving, supportive, and patient partner, Anis Sobhani, who let me ignore him (and domestic duties and our daughter) so I could interview, write, read, re-read, and complain. You are the one who keeps me steady.

Many thanks to my cool and collected editor, Jenny Bradshaw, who kept telling me I was almost there when I wasn't almost there; to my agent, Martha Webb at CookeMcDermid; to the whole team at McClelland & Stewart, especially Jared Bland, who heard Layton's story during a coffee date and immediately saw a book in it.

My dear friend Jennifer Yang not only came up with the book's title, but understood the heart of this story in a way no one else did and rescued it (and me) in more ways than I can count. Sarah Lilleyman and Jana Pruden are smart pals and even smarter editors who offered early feedback and cheerleading.

I have many friends who make me think about writing and life in new and challenging ways daily: Sarah Boesveld, Ellen Cobb-Friesen, Daniel Dale, Robyn Doolittle, Ann Hui, Lisan Jutras, Tim Kiladze, Michelle Li, Hannah Sung, and Carla Wintersgill.

Thank you to my family: Appa, Amma, and Anna. My in-laws, Zareen and Bassir Sobhani, housed me, fed me, chauffeured me, and loved me on all my many trips to Halifax.

A large portion of this book was written during two residencies at the Banff Centre for Arts and Creativity, a truly magical place. I am grateful to my cohorts from the 2014 Literary Journalism program, particularly my editor, Charlotte Gill, who helped shape so much of the earliest version of this story, and Ian Brown, who encouraged me to apply.

I appreciate all the editors at *The Globe and Mail* who gave me time for this side project, especially Christine Brousseau, Nicole MacIntyre, Angela Murphy, and Sinclair Stewart.

Thank you to Willie, Phil, Finn, Irma, and Matt for your patience, your honesty, and your faith in me.

To Candace: this might not have been what you signed up for, but in many ways this became your story, too. I can't thank you enough for everything, including your friendship.

Most of all: to Layton, who trusted me so fully with his story that he refused to read any version of it until it was published. I'm sorry you never got to see it in print, my friend, but I hope I haven't let you down.